LEARNING ROBOTS SUPPLY AND DEMAND SALE MARKET

JOHN LOK

Made with ♥ on the Notion Press Platform
www.notionpress.com

Contents

Preface

Introduction

In our societies , any kinds of products or services must need to apply demand and supply economic theory to analyze whether the kind of product or service may be value to invent to sell or serve to their customers in consumer market, if the kind of product or service demand number is less, then it ought not to raise manufacturing number to avoid "low price " sale or if the kind of product demand number is more, then it ought raise manufacturing number to have enough number in order to raise " high price" sale to satisfy customers their needs to buy their products.However, whether your product or serive's demand number depends on supply number or your product or service's supply number depends on demand number in order to make ths sale price is reasonable high or low level and reasonable supply number valuation.

In my this book, I shall indicate some actual product or service social suitation to explain whether these kinds of product or service is depended on either demand or supply aspect more in behavioral economic view, such as AI (artificial intelligence) or robot products whether their different kinds, such as cleaning robot, customer service robot, warehouse robot, even non-manual driving vehicle etc. products their demand will have how much demand in robot sale market as well as whether their supply will need to manufacture how much number in order to avoid sale prices are needed to be reduce.

Prologue

Contents

Chapter 1 Explaining supply and demand economic theory relationship

The difference between past and nowadays economists their demand and supply economic theory explanation?

What are the relationship between demand and supply?

p.3-20

Chapter 2 Human social job change demand and supply relationship

Why social behavior may influence organizational strategy needs to be changed p.21-51

Human Behavioral network job brings social
economic benefits

What does human network job mean

Why human network job behavior may influence economy

Robots take our jobs behavioral and economy influences

Robot job behavior brings economy influences

Chapter 3 Human intellectual demand and supply behavior relationship

Intellectual human economic behaviors p.52-74

What does intellectual human economic behaviors
mean ?

The relationship between social change and human
behavior

Chapter 4

Technology or human behavior whether may influence economic growth or recession

4 Why does (AI) big data gathering information technology influence the real market system change ?

5 Can (AI) big data gathering timing of information influence real marketing system?

6 (AI) big data gathering information can reduce the cost basis of economic activity to any businesses

7 The (AI) big data gathering technological innovation benefits

8 What is the relationship between the process of (AI) big data gathering technological innovation and the production of factor?

9 How to response times in (AI) manufacturing technological innovation?

10 Why technological innovation will be one factor of production to technological manufacture industry.

11 How can external and internal factors affect the product and (AI) manufacturing process innovation?

12 What is (AI) production of factor knowledge economy ?

13 (AI) Production of factor internal technical skill

14 What are the (AI) technical change as exogenous or endogenous production of factor?

Reference p.176-178

CHAPTER ONE

Explaining supply and demand economic theory relationship

The difference between past and nowadays economists their demand and supply economic theory explanation?

The law of supply and demand defines the relationship between the price of a given good or product and the willingness of people to either buy or sell it. Generally, as the price of a good increases, people are willing to supply more and demand less. These economists had explained economic demand and supply theory as below:

Philosopher John Locke is credited with one of the earliest written descriptions of this economic principle in his 1691 publication, Some Considerations of the Consequences of the Lowering of Interest and the Raising of the Value of Money. Locke addressed the concept of supply and demand as part of a discussion about interest rates in 17th-century England. Many merchants wanted the government to lower the cap on interest rates charged by private lenders so that people could borrow more money and thus purchase more goods. Locke argued that the free-market economy should set rates because government regulation could have unintended consequences. If the lending industry were left alone, interest rates would regulate themselves, Locke wrote: "The price of any commodity rises or falls by the proportion of the number of buyers and sellers."

Sir James Steuart's Inquiry into the Principles of Political Economy, published in 1796, was the first known printed use of the term "supply and demand." When Steuart wrote his treatise on political economy, one of his main concerns was the impact of supply and demand on laborers.

Adam Smith dealt extensively with the topic in his 1776 epic economic work, The Wealth of Nations. Often referred to as the Father of Economics, Smith explained the concept of supply and demand as an "invisible hand" that naturally guides the economy. According to Smith, the invisible hand is the automatic pricing and distribution mechanisms in the economy. Smith described a society in which bakers and butchers provide products that individuals need and want, providing a supply that meets demand and developing an economy that benefits everyone. It is important to note that Smith's ideas haven't gone without critique over the years since his ideas were first published, though. Over time, his ideas have been added to in order to represent the changing times and include concepts such as marginal utility, comparative advantage, entrepreneurship, the time-preference theory of interest, and monetary theory.

One of Marshall's most important contributions to microeconomics was his introduction of the concept of price elasticity of demand, which examines how price changes affect demand. In theory, people buy less of a particular product if the price increases, but Marshall noted that in real life, this behavior was not always true. The prices of some goods can increase without reducing demand, which means their prices are inelastic. Inelastic goods tend to include items such as medication or food that consumers deem crucial to daily life. Marshall argued that supply and demand, costs of production, and price elasticity all work together.

Nowadays economists they explain demand and supply economic theory, they have some different to past economists whose explanation as below:

How Does Supply and Demand Work? The law of supply and demand is a theory that explains the interaction between the sellers of a resource and the buyers of that resource. Generally, as price increases, people are willing to supply more and demand less and vice versa when the price falls. What does the bottom line mean. Despite the origins of the law of supply and demand beginning hundreds of years ago, it's still a topic frequently referenced and utilized today in economic theory and discussions. The theory has developed over time to accommodate recent technological and economical advancements, but the basic ideas of the theory remain largely the same.

Does demand depend on supply?

Supply and Demand Determine the Price of Goods and Quantities Produced and Consumed. Consumers may exhaust the available supply of a good by purchasing a given good or service at a high volume. This leads to an increase in demand. As demand increases, the available supply also decreases.

What does market demand depend on?

Market factors affecting demand of consumer goods. The demand for a good increases or decreases depending on several factors. This includes the product's price, perceived quality, advertising spend, consumer income, consumer confidence, and changes in taste and fashion.

Who controls the demand in supply and demand?

Supply and demand are in turn determined by technology and the conditions under which people operate. At one extreme, the market could be populated by a large number of virtually identical sellers and buyers (for example, the market for ballpoint pens).

What are the two laws of demand and supply?

The law of demand holds that the demand level for a product or a resource will decline as its price rises, and rise as the price drops. Conversely, the law of supply says higher prices boost supply of an economic good while lower ones tend to diminish it.

What factors affect demand and supply?

Price fluctuations are a strong factor affecting supply and demand.

When a product gets expensive enough that the average consumer no longer feels it is worth it to buy the product, then the demand declines. This leads to cuts in production that will hopefully stabilize the product's value.

What factors affect demand and demand?

Demand may be defined as the quantity of a commodity that a consumer is able and willing to buy, at each possible price, over a given period of time. ● Essential elements of demand are quantity, ability, willingness, prices, and period of time.

Which factors affect supply?

Generally, the supply of a product depends on its price and other variables such as the cost of production.

    a. Price. Price can be understood as what the consumer is willing to pay to receive a good or service. ...

b. Cost of production. ...

c. Technology. ...

d. Governments' policies. ...

e. Transportation condition.

How does supply and demand work together?

It's a fundamental economic principle that when supply exceeds demand for a good or service, prices fall. When demand exceeds supply, prices tend to rise. There is an inverse relationship between the supply and prices of goods and services when demand is unchanged.

What happens to supply when demand increases?

An increase in demand, all other things unchanged, will cause the equilibrium price to rise; quantity supplied will increase. A decrease in demand will cause the equilibrium price to fall; quantity supplied will decrease.

What is the theory of demand?

Demand theory describes the way that changes in the quantity of a good or service demanded by consumers affects its price in the market, The theory states that the higher the price of a product is, all else equal, the less of it will be demanded, inferring a downward sloping demand curve.

What are the 4 basic laws of supply and demand?
1) If the supply increases and demand stays the same, the price will go down. 2) If the supply decreases and demand stays the same, the price will go up. 3) If the supply stays the same and demand increases, the price will go up. 4) If the supply stays the same and demand decreases, the price will go down.

The different types of demand are as follows:

i. Individual and Market Demand: ...

ii. Organization and Industry Demand: ...

iii. Autonomous and Derived Demand: ...

iv. Demand for Perishable and Durable Goods: ...

v. Short-term and Long-term Demand:

What creates demand for a product?

You can create demand for a unique product if you can manage to solve a persistent problem for the consumer. People are always running away from pain, and providing them with an outlet is a sure-fire way to create massive demand for your goods.

What are the 7 factors that affect supply?

The seven factors which affect the changes of supply are as follows: (i) Natural Conditions (ii) Technical Progress (iii) Change in Factor Prices (iv) Transport Improvements (v) Calamities (vi) Monopolies (vii) Fiscal Policy.

What can affect demand?

Factors Affecting Demand

Price of the Product. ...

The Consumer's Income. ...

The Price of Related Goods. ...

The Tastes and Preferences of Consumers. ...

The Consumer's Expectations. ...

The Number of Consumers in the Market.

What are the three factors affecting demand?

The demand for a product will be influenced by several factors:

Price. Usually viewed as the most important factor that affects demand. ...

Income levels. ...

Consumer tastes and preferences. ...

Competition. ...

Fashions.

What are the 4 factors of supply?

The four factors that can shift the supply curve include natural conditions, input prices, technology, and government.

What causes increase in supply?

If the cost of production is lower, the profits available at a given price will increase, and producers will produce more. With more produced at every price, the supply curve will shift to the right, meaning an increase in supply.

What causes supply changes?

A change in supply is an economic term that describes when the suppliers of a given good or service alter production or output. A change in supply can occur as a result of new technologies, such as more efficient or less expensive production processes, or a change in the number of competitors in the market.

Is supply and demand a good strategy?

When it comes to profit placement, supply and demand zones can be a great tool as well. Always place your profit target ahead of a zone so that you don't risk giving back all your profits when the open interest in that zone is filled.

How is demand created?

Demand creation is a process that fuels the revenue pipeline so the sales team can meet or exceed their quotas. In other words, it takes your big idea — the creative appeal of your brand — and turns it into sales. That sounds a lot like demand generation, which often gets confused with lead generation.

What are the two parts of demand?

Economists define demand as the quantity of a good or service that buyers are willing and able to buy at all possible prices during a certain time period. Notice that there are two components to demand: willingness to purchase and ability to pay.

Can we control demand?

If you're willing to think and act strategically, you can easily manipulate the laws of supply and demand. It should be surprising to learn, however, that by manipulating the laws of supply and demand, you can make more profit in less time and with far fewer headaches

How do you control demand?

Here are five short-term actions to improve your demand variability management plans in this time of uncertainty:

Maintain transparent, proactive relationships with your suppliers. ...

Activate alternate sources of supply. ...

Reduce lead times. ...

Update inventory policy and planning. ...

Align supply and demand management.

What are the 8 types of demand?

There are 8 states of demand: negative demand, no demand, latent demand, falling demand, irregular demand, full demand, overfull demand and unwholesome demand.

What is Demand?

Types of Determinants of Demand. Every factor has a unique impact on demand. ...

Price of the Product. ...

The Income of the Consumers. ...

Number of Buyers in the Market. ...

Consumer's Expectations. ...

Tastes and Preferences of The Consumers. ...

Complement Goods. ...

Substitute Product.

What is theory of supply?

The law of supply is a fundamental principle of economic theory which states that, keeping other factors constant, an increase in price results in an increase in quantity supplied. In other words, there is a direct relationship between price and quantity: quantities respond in the same direction as price changes.

What are the types of supply?

There are five types of supply—market supply, short-term supply, long-term supply, joint supply, and composite supply.

Which comes first supply or demand?

Demand comes first and it's followed by the corresponding supplies. Supply and demand are both very important to economic activity. Supply is the total amount of a particular good or service available at a given time to consumers at a given price. Demand is a representation of a consumer's desire to purchase goods and services; it acts as a measurement of a consumer's willingness to purchase a specific good or service at a given price. These two economic forces influence each other; they are both important for the economy because they impact the prices of consumer goods and services within an economy and the quantities produced and consumed. Supply and demand are both keys to understanding the economy because they reflect the prices and quantities of consumer goods and services within an economy.

What are the relationship between demand and supply?

According to market economy theory, the relationship between supply and demand balances out at a point in the future; this point is called the equilibrium price.

Economists and companies analyze the relationship between supply and demand when making strategic product decisions. Both economists and companies analyze the relationship between supply and demand when making strategic product decisions. The assumption behind a market economy is that supply and demand are the best determinants for an economy's growth and health.

Consumer Behavior Influences Demand

One way that companies or economists might analyze this relationship is to create graphs that chart the equilibrium price of certain goods and services in order to determine product development and their production schedule. Consumer behavior dictates which products are produced and sold because consumers create the demand that companies attempt to meet. As a result, companies may study consumer behavior in an attempt to understand the current demand and predict future demand. It is vital that companies maintain the capacity to produce enough of a good or service that they can satisfy consumer demands.

Supply and demand are two sides of the same market coin. Generally, supply is how much of something is available or will be produced at a certain price. Demand is how much of something people want to purchase or consume at a certain price. One way to develop a more precise relationship between the two is to consider how the price of something affects its supply and its demand. Generally when the price of a good goes up, so does the supply, since firms are willing to create more when they can sell at higher prices. But when the price of a good goes up consumers will, at the same time, generally demand less. It is the interaction of supply and demand that determines how much will be produced and consumed and at what price, converging to a state known as equilibrium.

CHAPTER TWO

Human social job change demand and supply relationship

The difference between past and nowadays economists their demand and supply economic theory explanation?

The law of supply and demand defines the relationship between the price of a given good or product and the willingness of people to either buy or sell it. Generally, as the price of a good increases, people are willing to supply more and demand less. These economists had explained economic demand and supply theory as below:

Philosopher John Locke is credited with one of the earliest written descriptions of this economic principle in his 1691 publication, Some Considerations of the Consequences of the Lowering of Interest and the Raising of the Value of Money. Locke addressed the concept of supply and demand as part of a discussion about interest rates in 17th-century England. Many merchants wanted the government to lower the cap on interest rates charged by private lenders so that people could borrow more money and thus purchase more goods. Locke argued that the free-market economy should set rates because government regulation could have unintended consequences. If the lending industry were left alone, interest rates would regulate themselves, Locke wrote: "The price of any commodity rises or falls by the proportion of the number of buyers and sellers."

Sir James Steuart's Inquiry into the Principles of Political Economy, published in 1796, was the first known printed use of the term "supply and demand." When Steuart wrote his treatise on political economy, one of his main concerns was the impact of supply and demand on laborers.

Adam Smith dealt extensively with the topic in his 1776 epic economic work, The Wealth of Nations. Often referred to as the Father of Economics, Smith explained the concept of supply and demand as an "invisible hand" that naturally guides the economy. According to Smith, the invisible hand is the automatic pricing and distribution mechanisms in the economy. Smith described a society in which bakers and butchers provide products that individuals need and want, providing a supply that meets demand and developing an economy that benefits everyone. It is important to note that Smith's ideas haven't gone without critique over the years since his ideas were first published, though. Over time, his ideas have been added to in order to represent the changing times and include concepts such as marginal utility, comparative advantage, entrepreneurship, the time-preference theory of interest, and monetary theory.

One of Marshall's most important contributions to microeconomics was his introduction of the concept of price elasticity of demand, which examines how price changes affect demand. In theory, people buy less of a particular product if the price increases, but Marshall noted that in real life, this behavior was not always true. The prices of some goods can increase without reducing demand, which means their prices are inelastic. Inelastic goods tend to include items such as medication or food that consumers deem crucial to daily life. Marshall argued that supply and demand, costs of production, and price elasticity all work together.

Nowadays economists they explain demand and supply economic theory, they have some different to past economists whose explanation as below:

How Does Supply and Demand Work? The law of supply and demand is a theory that explains the interaction between the sellers of a resource and the buyers of that resource. Generally, as price increases, people are willing to supply more and demand less and vice versa when the price falls. What does the bottom line mean. Despite the origins of the law of supply and demand beginning hundreds of years ago, it's still a topic frequently referenced and utilized today in economic theory and discussions. The theory has developed over time to accommodate recent technological and economical advancements, but the basic ideas of the theory remain largely the same.

Does demand depend on supply?

Supply and Demand Determine the Price of Goods and Quantities Produced and Consumed. Consumers may exhaust the available supply of a good by purchasing a given good or service at a high volume. This leads to an increase in demand. As demand increases, the available supply also decreases.

What does market demand depend on?

Market factors affecting demand of consumer goods. The demand for a good increases or decreases depending on several factors. This includes the product's price, perceived quality, advertising spend, consumer income, consumer confidence, and changes in taste and fashion.

Who controls the demand in supply and demand?

Supply and demand are in turn determined by technology and the conditions under which people operate. At one extreme, the market could be populated by a large number of virtually identical sellers and buyers (for example, the market for ballpoint pens).

What are the two laws of demand and supply?

The law of demand holds that the demand level for a product or a resource will decline as its price rises, and rise as the price drops. Conversely, the law of supply says higher prices boost supply of an economic good while lower ones tend to diminish it.

What factors affect demand and supply?

Price fluctuations are a strong factor affecting supply and demand.

When a product gets expensive enough that the average consumer no longer feels it is worth it to buy the product, then the demand declines. This leads to cuts in production that will hopefully stabilize the product's value.

What factors affect demand and demand?

Demand may be defined as the quantity of a commodity that a consumer is able and willing to buy, at each possible price, over a given period of time. • Essential elements of demand are quantity, ability, willingness, prices, and period of time.

Which factors affect supply?

Generally, the supply of a product depends on its price and other variables such as the cost of production.

a. Price. Price can be understood as what the consumer is willing to pay to receive a good or service. ...

b. Cost of production. ...

c. Technology. ...

d. Governments' policies. ...

e. Transportation condition.

How does supply and demand work together?

It's a fundamental economic principle that when supply exceeds demand for a good or service, prices fall. When demand exceeds supply, prices tend to rise. There is an inverse relationship between the supply and prices of goods and services when demand is unchanged.

What happens to supply when demand increases?

An increase in demand, all other things unchanged, will cause the equilibrium price to rise; quantity supplied will increase. A decrease in demand will cause the equilibrium price to fall; quantity supplied will decrease.

What is the theory of demand?

Demand theory describes the way that changes in the quantity of a good or service demanded by consumers affects its price in the market, The theory states that the higher the price of a product is, all else equal, the less of it will be demanded, inferring a downward sloping demand curve.

What are the 4 basic laws of supply and demand?

1) If the supply increases and demand stays the same, the price will go down. 2) If the supply decreases and demand stays the same, the price will go up. 3) If the supply stays the same and demand increases, the price will go up. 4) If the supply stays the same and demand decreases, the price will go down.

The different types of demand are as follows:

i. Individual and Market Demand: ...

ii. Organization and Industry Demand: ...

iii. Autonomous and Derived Demand: ...

iv. Demand for Perishable and Durable Goods: ...

v. Short-term and Long-term Demand:

What creates demand for a product?

You can create demand for a unique product if you can manage to solve a persistent problem for the consumer. People are always running away from pain, and providing them with an outlet is a sure-fire way to create massive demand for your goods.

What are the 7 factors that affect supply?

The seven factors which affect the changes of supply are as follows: (i) Natural Conditions (ii) Technical Progress (iii) Change in Factor Prices (iv) Transport Improvements (v) Calamities (vi) Monopolies (vii) Fiscal Policy.

What can affect demand?

Factors Affecting Demand

Price of the Product. ...

The Consumer's Income. ...

The Price of Related Goods. ...

The Tastes and Preferences of Consumers. ...

The Consumer's Expectations. ...

The Number of Consumers in the Market.

What are the three factors affecting demand?

The demand for a product will be influenced by several factors:

Price. Usually viewed as the most important factor that affects demand. ...

Income levels. ...

Consumer tastes and preferences. ...
Competition. ...
Fashions.
What are the 4 factors of supply?
The four factors that can shift the supply curve include natural conditions, input prices, technology, and government.
What causes increase in supply?
If the cost of production is lower, the profits available at a given price will increase, and producers will produce more. With more produced at every price, the supply curve will shift to the right, meaning an increase in supply.
What causes supply changes?
A change in supply is an economic term that describes when the suppliers of a given good or service alter production or output. A change in supply can occur as a result of new technologies, such as more efficient or less expensive production processes, or a change in the number of competitors in the market.
Is supply and demand a good strategy?
When it comes to profit placement, supply and demand zones can be a great tool as well. Always place your profit target ahead of a zone so that you don't risk giving back all your profits when the open interest in that zone is filled.
How is demand created?
Demand creation is a process that fuels the revenue pipeline so the sales team can meet or exceed their quotas. In other words, it takes your big idea — the creative appeal of your brand — and turns it into sales. That sounds a lot like demand generation, which often gets confused with lead generation.
What are the two parts of demand?
Economists define demand as the quantity of a good or service that buyers are willing and able to buy at all possible prices during a certain time period. Notice that there are two components to demand: willingness to purchase and ability to pay.
Can we control demand?
If you're willing to think and act strategically, you can easily

manipulate the laws of supply and demand. It should be surprising to learn, however, that by manipulating the laws of supply and demand, you can make more profit in less time and with far fewer headaches

How do you control demand?

Here are five short-term actions to improve your demand variability management plans in this time of uncertainty:

Maintain transparent, proactive relationships with your suppliers. ...

Activate alternate sources of supply. ...

Reduce lead times. ...

Update inventory policy and planning. ...

Align supply and demand management.

What are the 8 types of demand?

There are 8 states of demand: negative demand, no demand, latent demand, falling demand, irregular demand, full demand, overfull demand and unwholesome demand.

What is Demand?

Types of Determinants of Demand. Every factor has a unique impact on demand. ...

Price of the Product. ...

The Income of the Consumers. ...

Number of Buyers in the Market. ...

Consumer's Expectations. ...

Tastes and Preferences of The Consumers. ...

Complement Goods. ...

Substitute Product.

What is theory of supply?

The law of supply is a fundamental principle of economic theory which states that, keeping other factors constant, an increase in price results in an increase in quantity supplied. In other words, there is a direct relationship between price and quantity: quantities respond in the same direction as price changes.

What are the types of supply?

There are five types of supply—market supply, short-term supply, long-term supply, joint supply, and composite supply.

Which comes first supply or demand?

Demand comes first and it's followed by the corresponding supplies. Supply and demand are both very important to economic activity. Supply is the total amount of a particular good or service available at a given time to consumers at a given price. Demand is a representation of a consumer's desire to purchase goods and services; it acts as a measurement of a consumer's willingness to purchase a specific good or service at a given price. These two economic forces influence each other; they are both important for the economy because they impact the prices of consumer goods and services within an economy and the quantities produced and consumed. Supply and demand are both keys to understanding the economy because they reflect the prices and quantities of consumer goods and services within an economy.

What are the relationship between demand and supply?

According to market economy theory, the relationship between supply and demand balances out at a point in the future; this point is called the equilibrium price.

Economists and companies analyze the relationship between supply and demand when making strategic product decisions. Both economists and companies analyze the relationship between supply and demand when making strategic product decisions. The assumption behind a market economy is that supply and demand are the best determinants for an economy's growth and health.

Consumer Behavior Influences Demand

One way that companies or economists might analyze this relationship is to create graphs that chart the equilibrium price of certain goods and services in order to determine product development and their production schedule. Consumer behavior dictates which products are produced and sold because consumers create the demand that companies attempt to meet. As a result, companies may study consumer behavior in an attempt to understand the current demand and predict future demand. It is vital that companies maintain the capacity to produce enough of a good or service that they can satisfy consumer demands.

Supply and demand are two sides of the same market coin. Generally, supply is how much of something is available or will be produced at a certain price. Demand is how much of something people want to purchase or consume at a certain price. One way to develop a more precise relationship between the two is to consider how the price of something affects its supply and its demand. Generally when the price of a good goes up, so does the supply, since firms are willing to create more when they can sell at higher prices. But when the price of a good goes up consumers will, at the same time, generally demand less. It is the interaction of supply and demand that determines how much will be produced and consumed and at what price, converging to a state known as equilibrium.

Human intellectual demand and supply behavior relationship

Intellectual human economic behaviors

What does intellectual human economic behaviors mean ? Human foolish behavior is depended on social enjoyment need more or material social supply more? I believe that when we choose or decide to do intellectual behaviors, then our societies will be influenced to bring economic growth in consequence.I shall attempt to indicate pollution case to explain how and why eithet our intellectual or foolish behaviors may bring economic growth or recession in consequence as below:

On one hand, for air pollution social case aspect example, if we only consider to buy cars to drive for working aim or holiday leisure aim. Then, our societies air will be polluted. Our health will be influenced to bad. Our car driving behaviors may cause global environment air pollution serously. In long tiem, global air pollution will bring our bodies health to be bad. Although, ourselves car driving behaviors may bring our driving travelling leisure enjoyment and comfortable feeling in short time, also we so not need to pay public transport fare often, but we need to compensate ourselves health economic intangible loss due to air pollution , when cars number increases, dirty air will cause ouselves health to become bad.

In the result, we will need to pay more medical expenditure when we are old age, due to ourselves bodies will become bad, due to we breathe global dirty air every day, due to ourselves cars pollute air in long time, e.g. 10 to 20 years, even 30 more without limited air pollution environment. So, driving cars behavior may be one kind of human foolish behavior and our foolish behavior may bring ourselves future long time medical expenditure absolutely.

One the other hand, water pollution social aspect, if we often keep much rubblish to pollute sea, oil exploration porcessing pollute ocean , ships gas pollute ocaen, then fishes will eat polluted food and drive dirty water, due to global ocean is polluted.

In fact, because human only to conside how to buy boats to carry on leisure enjoyment activities, or catch cruises to travel on the sea. Also, oil manufacturers only consider researching anywhere to find new oil exploration places to manufacture oil product, when their oil exploration processes pollute ocarn . Consequently, global fishes drink polluted warer or eat polluted food. They will have poison. SO, human will have high chance to eat poison polluted fishes, due to fishes are poison or are polluted.

So, human is doing foolish activities, we only hope to find oil exploration places to pollute ocean or we only spend money to buy ticket to catch ships to travel anywhere in global ocean. All of these human foolish behaviors will bring pollution to global ocean. On consequently, we will need to compensate to eat polluted or dirty or poision fishes, ourselves bodies health will be bad. In long time, we need have high chance to pay medical expenditure when we are old. So, pollution case may be one good example to explain how and why human foolish behavior may influence ourselves future need to compensate serious medical loss.

All of these human foolish behavior will bring pollution to global ocean. On consequently, we will need to compensate to eat polluted or dirty or poison fished , ourselves bodies health will be bad. In long time, we will have high chance to pay medical expenditure, when we are old. So, pollution case may be one good example to explain how and why human ourselves intellectual or foolish behaviors may influence future long time economic loss or economic growth or recession in micro and micro economic view.

On another water pollution aspect hand, if we often keep rubbish to sea, oil exploration processing pollutes ocean and ships' gas pollute ocean, then fishes will eat polluted food and drink dirty water, due to fishes will eat polluted food and drink dirty sea water because the global ocean is polluted seriously.

In fact, because human only consider how to buy boats to carry on any leisure water activities, or catches cruises to travel on the sea. Also, oil manufacturers only consider any where to find oil exploratin places to manufacture oil products from ocean, when their pol exploration processes can plooute ocean. Consequently, global fishes drink polluted water or eat direty food. They will have poison. So, human will have high chance to eat poison fishes.

Otherwise, such as pollutin case, it can infuence inflation or deflation. Consequently, the reason indicates supply and demand theory. If air pollution is serious, then we will consider health issue, global cars demand number may be influenced to reduce, when global cars number demand will reduce, global car prices and supply number will need to change to fall down in order to attract or persuade global car consumers choose to make car purchase decision.

Hence, global car manufacture number and car price will be influenced to reduce, due to global air pollution issue. Consequently, deflation will occur because when the country citizen usually does not spend much extra saving money to buy car expensive goods. Money value will be low. Otherwise, if global cair pollution is not serious, human considers to buy cars to enjoy driving leisure lives. So, global car demand is influenced to increase , also global car price will also influenced to increase.

Consequently, gobal human will choose to buy cars to drive. Due to we accept to spend extra saving to buy expensive car goods. Car sale price and supply may be influenced to rise up. Money value is influenced to reduce. Inflation may be influenced, due to global car consumers number increases, we would not have extra money to spend easily. Car expensive goods expenditure influences our spending habit to avoid to make car purchase decision more easily. So, human intellectual or foolish activities may bring inflation or deflation consequency in possible indirectly in macro economic view.

On conclusion, above pollution case explain that how and why human intellectual or foolish economic behaviors may bring inflation or deflation consequency as wll as economic growth or recession consequency as well as any goods demand and supply increasing or decreasing consequency. It implies that human behavior may have indirect relationship to influence any goods demand and supply number to either increase or decrease result as well as any goods price will be influenced to increase or decrease in micro and macro economic view. Hence, Human foolish behavior is depended on social enjoyment need more or material social supply more because human needs to raise enjoyment feel , so we will choose to do foolish behavior, e.g. air pollution, when many people choose to buy cars to drive to replace catch public transport. So, such as car market, it depends on car demand number more than car supply number absolutely in demand and supply view.

The relationship between social change and human behavior

Why does economic changes may influence human individual behavioral change? I shall attempt to indicate shopping behavior and staying at home behavior to explain their case and effect relationsip as below:

Human behavior can be influenced by economic change or economic change can be influenced by human behavior? Why does recession may influence consumers reduce shopping desire? In social recession suitation, it is possible that many people lose jobs suddenly, due to businessmen lose many customers. They need to make decision to reduce employees number in order to continue to keep businesses. Consequently, many firms (organizations) their employees may lose jobs. When they have much time, due to lose jobs, they will feel to avoid to spend too much time and money to go to shopping often. Many losing jobs people, they will often stay at homes.

So, they will reduce time to go to shopping, then non essential products won't their preferable choice purchase products. Hence, recession will change many losing jobs people their shopping or consumption desires to avoid to buy non essential products often . Usually when economic boom, many people have jobs to do because consumers number must increase when many people have jobs to do. Then, many people can accept to spend money to buy non essential products often. Many people feel spend time to go to shopping can satisfy their purchase of any kinds of new products useful psychology or desire. So, recession is one good example to explain it can influence many people do not like often to leave homes to go to shopping easily. Many people like to stay at homes, becaue they feel worry about spending too much shopping time when they leave homes. Their staying home time is one good negative shopping behavior example. So, economic change may influence human individual behavior changes , they have direct cause and efect relationship in behavioral economic view.

May human behavior influence economic change? Is it possible that human behavior may bring the country social economic change in macro economic or micro behavioral economic view ? I shall indicate publishing industry example. Do you feel that if there are many students feel learning is very important when they read many books or many of students feel interesting to read or they have reading new books in habit, then it is possible that the country will have many students like to spend time to go to any book shops to choose the books, they feel that they can help they learn new knowledge. Then the country will increase students number, they often spend time to visit any one book shop every week. Their visiting book shops behavior which may become their habits. So, the country will increase students number, they often spend time to visit book shops. Also, it implies that visiting book shops behaviors may be their behavioral habits.

So, when the country has many students often spend time to visit book shops , their visiting book shops behaviors may help any one book shop to raise books sale chance. So, the country's student individual often visiting book shop behaviors, their habitual visiting book shops behaviors must may assist help any one book shop to increase books sale number absolutely.

Consequently, any one book shop , its books sale bumber must be influenced to increase to increase because the country will have many students like or feel need visit book shops habit in order to choose any suitable books to buy to read at home in order to raise themselves learning effort. When the country has many bok shops often have many students visit their book shops, then their books sale number may be influenced to increase. It explain why student individual visiting book shop behavior may help any one book shop sale number increases also. So, visiting shops products sale number is depended on online products supply number, if online products supply number increases, then it may cause many customers choose to buy the kind of products from online webstore. So, any shop products sale number will depend on onlint products supply number in supply and demand view.

CHAPTER FOUR

Technology or human behavior whether may influence economic growth or recession

Human Behavioral network job brings social economic benefits

What does human network job mean ? Why may human network job be popular? Why human network job behavior may influence economy ?

Nowadays internet is popular to use. We can apply internet to find data , search any new things, even earn money. Why does internet may become huma network job source. For example, e-publish may be one kind of new human network job. Any authors may apply internet

channel to help them to sell electronic or paper books from e-publisher web store. They may apply facebook, you tub etc. any online

channel to promote themselves new books to let new readers to know whether when they may buy themselves favourable new topic books to read

from electronic publisher web store.

Thus, future electronic publisher industry may help any authors to build internet network platform to help them to sell and promote ot advertise their any one new electronic or paper book topic to let global any one reader to choose to buy their any new topic books from electronic publisher web store easily and conveniently. However, it implies that electronic network platform author may be one kind of future new human network job in our societies.

How electronic network platform author job may bring economy benefit in macro economy view? A person can have few friends, contacts and still be very influential if these few friends and contacts are themselves highly influential, e.g. one author must not need to know any one reader in global society. When they like to choose any electronic books from electronic internet network platform. They may become the author's any one topic book buyer, when they feel the author's any one topic book is fun and attract they make decision to buth the strange author whose the topic book from electronic book publisher's platform web store conventiently in short time. Although, they are strangers, they do not know themselves , but the reader can understand what it way that made Google from writing platofrm to create new creative mind and typing network job method to replace traditional hand writing book method for global authors. It will be one kind of new human network writing job.

Hence, global any one reader can apply an innovative search engine , such as google.com to find whether whom author personal new topic books are value to read from internet.

Then, the electroniuc publisher's web store may be new book store platform sale network to help the author to sell many electronic or paper books from electronic network platform in short time. So, internet may be future new network plaform to help global any one author to create network writing job absolutely. Furthermore, internet may be popular social media to help any one author to build goold relationship between his/ her readers. It is one kind of new network, human network job. New authors do not need to buy many paper books to prepare to put in any one book shop warehouse. Their every book can print on demand to reduce out of book stock in any one book shop. They may choose to sell either electronic books or paper books both from any one book publisher web store. So, electronic network platform may be one kind of good writing channel to help human authors to create income and it can also help authors to bring new creative mind and new topic fun content books to let readers to know and buy to read from electronic publisher network platform.

Why does human behavior may be one kind of new human network job to bring global economic advantages. ALthough, it may be free income or without inocme, but the person does the network behavior, his/her behavior may be bring advantages to influence many other people's health. For this case, when a worker in a coffee shop in an airport gets a vaccination aganinst the flu, it does not only helps him or her stay healthy, but also helps the many travellers who might otherwise have been inflected if that workers caught the flu. So, the externality , the result implies the vaccination of even a part of a community conveys benefits to the whole community. For example, governments pay special attention to the vaccinations of school children, teachers, health mothers, and the elderly, categories of people particularly susceptible not only to catching, but also to transmitting a disease.

It is not accidential that governments are heavily involved with vaccination . When there are externalities, free market, fail to persuade individual incentives with society's
their the worker's decision of whether to get a vaccine ends up attracting whether other people get sick. The workers might not fully take all these other people's potential suffering into account when making her or his vaccination decision.

As Stanford University does many suggestions, understand this and tries to help them make the right decisions and so providers free flu vaccines for its staff and students.
Small pockets of unvaccinated individuals can allow a disease to gain a spread more widely well-being. For example, parent weighing the costs and benefits of a vaccine for their child is not always

thinking of the consequences of that vaccination to other people. THese are markets in which subsidizing or regulating behavior can make everyone better off. Because the reason for requiring that a child be vaccinated before enrolling in school is not just to protect that child, because each child's vaccination affects others via potential contagions.

Robots take our jobs behavioral and economy influences

Robot job behavior brings economy influences

If one day robots can replace human to do simple, even complex jobs. They will bring what influences to our global societial economy.The popular economic refrain declares that the

global middle class is dying and robots will soon take our jobs, e.g. shopping center customer service jobs, library service jobs, cinema ticket sale jobs, restaurant kitchen cooker jobs,

even, bus drivers, taxi drivers etc. public transport driving jobs, accountant, doctors etc. professional jobs. Whether it is beautiful or petty matter if our future societies have many human jobs can be replaced to do from robots. Businessman must may reduce to employ employees and reduce to pay salary or wage, when robots can be replaced to do their employees tasks. But, societies must bring unemployement rate rises , due to societies will have many people loss jobs when their employers choose to buy robots to serve their clients or do any office tasks or customer service or cleaning etc. tasks.

In micro economy view, employers may save money in long term, but in macro economy view, it will cause unemployment ratio rises , even crime rate rises when there are many people lose

jobs in societies. These models of doom, though, fail to account for the hundreds of businesses riding the waves of change in their industries when robots may be invented to replace human to do many simple , even complex tasks in our future societies.

WE may image that one small factory needs to manufacture fishes canes to sell to supermarket, the small , cheaper stuff and higher margin parts of the fishes manufacture industry. Before, this factory needs to employe many human factory workers need to help every fresh customer makeing the perfect fishing gear, designed for performance, durability, and cost in order to achieve to manufacture every fish cane in whole fished processing manufacturing stages. Every worker needs to spend about 15 to twenty minutes to finish every fish cane , till to delivery to any supermarket to sell. If this fish canes manufacturing factory can apply manufacturing robots to help them to finish any one working tasks , every robot can only spend five minutes to finish whole fresh fish cane manufacturing process. Thus, every robot can

help this factory save 10 to 15 minutes time to finsh every fish cane manufacturing process. IN fact, time is money, because when every robot can help this factory to reduce 10 to 15 minutes time to compare human worker. Then, this factory can finish about 20 fish canes in one hour if it can use robot to help it to manufacture fish canes. Otherwise, if this factory still use human workers to help it to manufacture fish canes, then it can finsh about 3 to 4 fish canes in one hour. SO, the manufacturing efficiency ensures that robots must help this fish manufacturing factory to raise fish canes number more than human workers. So, in robotic behavioral economy view, manufacturing robots must help this fish canes manufacturing factory to raise fish canes manufacturing number and deliver increasing number to supermarkets to prepare to sell every day. Robots can help this fish canes manufacturing factory bring manufacturing time saving, rising manufacturing efficiency, improving performance and reducing wages expenditure long time advantages in micro economy view. However, manufacturing robots can also bring disadvanages to society, e.g. increasing unemployment ratio, increasing crime rate,

this factory workers will lose jobs and income, they need earn social welfare from government and increasing government finance pressure in short time, even long time in macro economic view.

Stanford University graduate program in economics, Scott lecturer explained that "in demand and supply economic theory for robots supply and demand case, robots supply number increasing may influence human workers demand number decrease. It sometimes calls " the efficient frontier".

No specific human beings were mentioned in any of economics classes. As robots supply and demand in market case, They (robots) may be purely theoretical " agents" who reached to the most reasonable sale prices in order to persuade any one businessman buyer to make manufacturing robot buying decision whether robots can help him / her to bring how much saving time , saving money, saving cost, improving performance, efficiency economic benefit before he/she plans to reduce workers number when he/she decides to apply robots to replace human workers in his/her factory or office or any service department, e.g. cinema ticket sale service, shopping center customer service, shopping center cleaning , supermarket customer service etc. service or sale tasks. When robots can replace human to do any one of these tasks in any organizations. So, robots may be human worker agents who reached to prices the way robots would react to a software

command. There was nothing that explained why some people thrived and others did n't or why truly brilliant, hardworking people could fail when much lazier folks succeeded." Having been admitted to the Stanford University graduate program in economics, Scott lecturer hoped to get his answers there.

How robots influence our future social changing? Using the right technology can be a boon to your business in this economy. For internet example, it is easier than ever to find well-matched customers all around the world, to stay in contact with them, and to more quickly design the products they want. If you focus solely on being cutting -edge, though you risk letting the technology

take over what should be very robust relationships with your customers , employees, and colleagues. IN nowaddays society, technoligical advances and cutomation, personal

relationships in business are more crucial than ever. I mean that robots can not replace human to serve clients to let them to feel more comfortable and passion more easily. For shoe shop case example, if the shoe shop apply one robot to serve its clients to

replace human shoe salesperson to serve its shoe customers. Robots ensure that they can not persuade every shoe potential buyer to make shoe buying decision more easily when robots need to contact every shoe potential buyer. The reason is simple, because robots can not touch any one shoe buyer individual emotion very easier.
If the shoe buyer needs the robots to help him/her to choose any right shoe styles when he/she can not feel himself / herself can make the most right shoe style choice decision. The robots can not replace human shoe salesperson to make shoe style choice judgement more easily. They must need longer time to analyze whether which shoe style may be the most suitable to the shoe buyer. Otherwise, human shoe salesperson may attempt to make the most right shoe style choice decision to help any one shoe buyer to chooce the most right style shoe because he/she owns shoe style sale experience, shoe style knowledge, the most important reason is that they can feel every shoe customer individual emotion to touch whether he/she will feel comfortable or happy when they attempt to help every shoe customer to seek the most right shoe style in every shoe customer whole shoe searching processing. Othwerwise, serving robots are only one machine, they can not touch or feel every shoe customer individual emotion whether he/she feel comfortable or unhappy or happy when they need to contact them in whole shoe searching processing. Hence, I believe that some tasks robots can
not repalce human staff to do very easily. Otherwise, robots may bring disadvanatges to let any one businessman to loss his/her customers, due to robots can not touch every customer
emotion to compare human staff in service tasks more easily. Robots serving customer behaviors may cause money lose and customers number lose to the shop in micro economic view.

   Intellectual human economic behaviors
What does intellectual human economic behaviors mean ? I believe that when we choose or decide to do intellectual behaviors, then our societies will be influenced to bring economic growth in consequence.I shall attempt to indicate pollution case to explain

how and why eithet our intellectual or foolish behaviors may bring economic growth or recession in consequence as below:

On one hand, for air pollution social case aspect example, if we only consider to buy cars to drive for working aimr or holiday leisure aim. Then, our societies air will be polluted. Our health will be influenced to bad. Our car driving behaviors may cause global environment air pollution serously. In long tiem, global air pollution will bring our bodies health to be bad. Although, ourselves car driving behaviors may bring our driving travelling leisure enjoyment and comfortable feeling in short time, also we so not need to pay public transport fare often, but we need to compensate ourselves health economic intangible loss due to air pollution , when cars number increases, dirty air will cause ouselves health to become bad.

In the result, we will need to pay more medical expenditure when we are old age, due to ourselves bodies will become bad, due to we breathe global dirty air every day, due to ourselves cars pollute air in long time, e.g. 10 to 20 years, even 30 more without limited air pollution environment. So, driving cars behavior may be one kind of human foolish behavior and our foolish behavior may bring ourselves future long time medical expenditure absolutely.

One the other hand, water pollution social aspect, if we often keep much rubblish to pollute sea, oil exploration porcessing pollute ocean , ships gas pollute ocaen, then fishes will eat polluted food and drive dirty water, due to global ocean is polluted.

In fact, because human only to conside how to buy boats to carry on leisure enjoyment activities, or catch cruises to travel on the sea. Also, oil manufacturers only consider researching anywhere to find new oil exploration places to manufacture oil product, when their oil exploration processes pollute ocarn . Consequently, global fishes drink polluted warer or eat polluted food. They will have poison. SO, human will have high chance to eat poison polluted fishes, due to fishes are poison or are polluted.

So, human is doing foolish activities, we only hope to find oil exploration places to pollute ocean or we only spend money to buy ticket to catch ships to travel anywhere in global ocean. All of these human foolish behaviors will bring pollution to global ocean. On consequently, we will need to compensate to eat polluted or dirty or poision fishes, ourselves bodies health will be bad. In long time, we need have high chance to pay medical expenditure when we are old. So, pollution case may be one good example to explain how and why human foolish behavior may influence ourselves future need to compensate serious medical loss.

All of these human foolish behavior will bring pollution to global ocean. On consequently, we will need to compensate to eat polluted or dirty or poison fished , ourselves bodies health will be bad. In long time, we will have high chance to pay medical expenditure, when we are old. So, pollution case may be one good example to explain how and why human ourselves intellectual or foolish behaviors may influence future long time economic loss or economic growth or recession in micro and micro economic view.

On another water pollution aspect hand, if we often keep rubbish to sea, oil exploration processing pollutes ocean and ships' gas pollute ocean, then fishes will eat polluted food and drink dirty water, due to fishes will eat polluted food and drink dirty sea water because the global ocean is polluted seriously.

In fact, because human only consider how to buy boats to carry on any leisure water activities, or catches cruises to travel on the sea. Also, oil manufacturers only consider any where to find oil exploratin places to manufacture oil products from ocean, when their pol exploration processes can plooute ocean. Consequently, global fishes drink polluted water or eat direty food. They will have poison. So, human will have high chance to eat poison fishes.

Otherwise, such as pollutin case, it can infuence inflation or deflation. Consequently, the reason indicates supply and demand theory. If air pollution is serious, then we will consider health issue, global cars demand number may be influenced to reduce, when global cars number demand will reduce, global car prices and supply number will need to change to fall down in order to attract or persuade global car consumers choose to make car purchase decision.

Hence, global car manufacture number and car price will be influenced to reduce, due to global air pollution issue. Consequently, deflation will occur because when the country citizen usually does not spend much extra saving money to buy car expensive goods. Money value will be low. Otherwise, if global cair pollution is not serious, human considers to buy cars to enjoy driving leisure lives. So, global car demand is influenced to increase , also global car price will also influenced to increase.

Consequently, gobal human will choose to buy cars to drive. Due to we accept to spend extra saving to buy expensive car goods. Car sale price and supply may be influenced to rise up. Money value is influenced to reduce. Inflation may be influenced, due to global car consumers number increases, we would not have extra money to spend easily. Car expensive goods expenditure influences our spending habit to avoid to make car purchase decision more easily. So, human intellectual or foolish activities may bring inflation or deflation consequency in possible indirectly in macro economic view.

On conclusion, above pollution case explain that how and why human intellectual or foolish economic behaviors may bring inflation or deflation consequency as wll as economic growth or recession consequency as well as any goods demand and supply increasing or decreasing consequency. It implies that human behavior may have indirect relationship to influence any goods demand and supply number to either increase or decrease result as well as any goods price will be influenced to increase or decrease in micro and macro economic view.

The relationship between social change and human behavior

Why does economic changes may influence human individual behavioral change? I shall attempt to indicate shopping behavior and staying at home behavior to explain their case and effect relationsip as below:

Human behavior can be influenced by economic change or economic change can be influenced by human behavior? Why does recession may influence consumers reduce shopping desire? In social recession suitation, it is possible that many people lose jobs suddenly, due to businessmen lose many customers. They need to make decision to reduce employees number in order to continue to keep businesses. Consequently, many firms (organizations) their employees may lose jobs. When they have much time, due to lose jobs, they will feel to avoid to spend too much time and money to go to shopping often. Many losing jobs people, they will often stay at homes.

So, they will reduce time to go to shopping, then non essential products won't their preferable choice purchase products. Hence, recession will change many losing jobs people their shopping or consumption desires to avoid to buy non essential products often . Usually when economic boom, many people have jobs to do because consumers number must increase when many people have jobs to do. Then, many people can accept to spend money to buy non essential products often. Many people feel spend time to go to shopping can satisfy their purchase of any kinds of new products useful psychology or desire. So, recession is one good example to explain it can influence many people do not like often to leave homes to go to shopping easily. Many people like to stay at homes, becaue they feel worry about spending too much shopping time when they leave homes. Their staying home time is one good negative shopping behavior example. So, economic change may influence human individual behavior changes , they have direct cause and efect relationship in behavioral economic view.

May human behavior influence economic change? Is it possible that human behavior may bring the country social economic change in macro economic or micro behavioral economic view ? I shall indicate publishing industry example. Do you feel that if there are many students feel learning is very important when they read many books or many of students feel interesting to read or they have reading new books in habit, then it is possible that the country will have many students like to spend time to go to any book shops to choose the books, they feel that they can help they learn new knowledge. Then the country will increase students number, they often spend time to visit any one book shop every week. Their visiting book shops behavior which may become their habits. So, the country will increase students number, they often spend time to visit book shops. Also, it implies that visiting book shops behaviors may be their behavioral habits.

So, when the country has many students often spend time to visit book shops , their visiting book shops behaviors may help any one book shop to raise books sale chance. So, the country's student individual often visiting book shop behaviors, their habitual visiting book shops behaviors must may assist help any one book shop to increase books sale number absolutely.

Consequently, any one book shop , its books sale bumber must be influenced to increase to increase because the country will have many students like or feel need visit book shops habit in order to choose any suitable books to buy to read at home in order to raise themselves learning effort. When the country has many bok shops often have many students visit their book shops, then their books sale number may be influenced to increase. It explain why student individual visiting book shop behavior may help any one book shop sale number increases also.

How human productive behavior may influence economic development

May any country which citizen behavior assist themselves country development? It is one cause and effect economic question. I mean that if the country itself citicen can not concentrate mind or energy to choose to do one kind of industry in order to let themselves country can bring the most benefit, then whether the counry itself economy can bring the most serious economic benefit. I shall attempt to indicate these countries themselves indistry choice to explain whether these countries themselves citizen productive behavior may help themselves countries to achieve the largest economic benefits. I shall indicate as below:

New Zealand farmer individual wine productive behavior

For New Zealand country example, this country concerns itself effort is foucs on farming agricultural aspect. So, this country has many farmers concentrate on farming agricultural aspect. May New Zealanders choose to spend time to produce different kinds of wines, e.g. wine or red grape wine is for the people are eating meat, or they are eating dinner.

When these New Zealanders their behaviors choose to do farming or agriculture to grow and produce different kinds of taste of white or red grape wine drinking products job. Themselves grape agriculture behavior will influence these New Zealanders themselves, they can learn how to improve different kinds of grape wine drinking products in order to achieve every kinds of white or read grape wines taste improving aim during their white or red grape producing process.

Why can New Zealander every individual white or read grape wine producers improve their white or read grape wine taste more easily? In behavioral economic view, it can explain that why any one New Zealander white or read grape wine producer can be encouraged or excited or persuaded to concentrate nervous and energy and effort to learn how to improve their white or red grape wine products easily.

In fact, New Zealand is one agricultural food export country. It has good natural environment resource , e.g. land, seed to provide any one farmer to produce themselves any kinds of agricultrual food products, e.g. fruit, or wine food products. Because New Zealanders know themselves country has enough natural resource . So, in common, many New Zealanders choose to attempt to do farming agricultural jobs in order to export themselves any kinds of fruit or meat or wine products to overseas or sell to domestic in order to earn profit.

So, when these New Zealand farmers number has been increasing every year. This country farmers will feel themsleves competition between this New Zealand farmers themselves are serious due to they may feel New Zealanders choose to do agriculture businesses in order to export themselves different kinds of farming food to overseas or sell to local to earn profit.

Hence, when many New Zealand farmers feel that farmers number has been increasing every year. They will feel themselves competition is serious. They must need to spend much time and nervous and effort to research what method is the best how to produce the best taste of white or red grape wine products in order to let local or overseas wine buyers to choose to buy his/her producing white or read grpae products to drink.

Hence, in competition psychological view, may influence many New Zealand white or reaad wine producers had been beginning to change their learning behavior on researching what method is the best in order to produce the best quality of taste red or white wine products to sell in order to attract overseas or local white or read grape wine drinkers to choose to buy his/her wine products. Their behavior will focus on learning how to raising or improving white or read grape wine taste method more than only focus on producing a large number white or red grape wine products. They believe wine quality is more important to compare wine producing number. So, New Zealand wine producers themselves wine producers behaviors have been changing on concentrating on researching wine quality method aspect more then wine producing number aspect in behavioral economic view.

America high technological productive behavior

For America example, US is one high technological country, it owns many high technological knowledge talent inventors, e.g. computer science inventors. Hence, US must attract many diferent countries owning high technological computer inventors choose to go to US to develop their computer science profession career. Also, it seems that when many computer science inventors or professions choose to go to US to develop themselves computer science new career. In behavioral economic view, due to their leaving themselves countries choice, which may bring influence themselve country job behaviors need to be changed. They must need to adapt US new live. Because they will forgive their past computer science job. These computer science professionals need to spend time to adapt US new lives. They " past computer science job behaviors" will need to be changed to their new US any computer employer's new computer science job model.

Because their traditional computer science jobs needed to be forgot in their themselves countries. They will feel their old computer science job knowledge and behavior needed to change in order to let their US any one new of computer company employer feels satisfactory to accept their new working behavior in any one US computer organization.

So, on the other hand, many US computer company employer will feel that they must need time to accept any one new overseas computer science professions their working behaviors, their working attitude daily, because these foreign comouter science professional, their past computer working behaviors and working attitude must be different to US domestic computer science professions.

In behavioral economic view, these overseas computer science professions, their working behaviors and attitude must be needed to change in order to adapt any one US new computer company itself domestic or local computer science professional stafs themselves daily working behaviors and attitude because these overseas and local computer science professionals must need to team work together.

In behavioral economic view, it is only one way that foreign computer science professionals must need to change themselves past country traditiona daily working behaviors and attitude in order to cooperate with these US local computer science professionals in teams more easily.

Consequently, if these foreign compute science professionals can change their past working behaviors and attitude to let any one US local computer science professional feels to cooperate with them easily in short time. Then, the US computer company itself whole computer professional teams themselves efficiencies will be influenced to raised or improved by the changing past working attitude and working behaviors of these foreign computer science professionals. So, in behavioral economic view, only if US any one computer company hopes itself computer teams themselves efficiency can be raised or improved when it decides to employ foreign computer science professionals and US domestic computer science professionals. They need to work in teams together. They must need to let these foreign computer science professionals to know how to change their working behaviors and attitude to let their domestic computer science professionals feel easy to work together. Then, the US computer company itself whole team efficiency must be rasied or improved easily in short time.

● China share market investing behavior

For China share market example, economic development depends on financial market. Because if many Chinese have interest to invest to carry on shares buying and selling activities in orde to learn how to earn shares interest and share profit when the China shareholder can make decision to sell himself/herself shares in the the high price, then he/she can earn money when he/she can sell the China company's shares in the high sale share price position.

If China has many Chinese like to spend time to carry on investing shares activities. Themselves shares buying and selling behaviors will influence China has many companies can increase fund from many Chinese shareholders in order to have enough money to expand or develop themselves businesses in China in long term.

Consequently, when China can have many Chinese like to attempt to carry on buying and selling shares investing behaviors in China share market. Themselves buying and selling shares behaviors can help many Chinese companies have effort to increase enough money or capital in order to continue to do their businesses in long term absolutely. So, it explains why when many Chinese become shareholders , they can assist China will have many companies continue to develop their businesses if many Chinese like to carry on shares buying and selling investing behaviors in long time in China financial investment market nowadays in behavioral economic view.

Why has any individual country have many people invest share behavior which can influence the country's macro consumption desire?

I shall apply shares market buying and selling investment behavior to explaiin why shares investment behavior which may impact the country's overal consumption desire as below:

In behavioral economic view, I assume that when the coutry has many people have interest to attempt to carry on shares buying and selling investment behavior, then their frequent shares buying and selling behaviors which may bring negactive consumption desire or shopping desire of these shares investors their consumer behavior. The reason is simple, when the country has many share buyers number suddenly been increasing rapidly. Consequently, these large group share investors must need to spend much time to research any kinds of company shares variations, whether when their share prices will rise up of fall down in order to achieve buying the company's shares in the lowest price and selling the company's shares in the highest price level in order to earn profit.

Basic on this reason, they must need to spend much extra time to research share prices changing behavior every day, e.g. one working person will wait to leave his/her job, after he/she can spend time to gather data to research the day's share price changing behavior after dinner. So, the working person's right time may be his/her share price market research behavior. Before he/she may spend his/her night time to go to shopping after dinner, but nowadays, he/she will fogive to do his/her shopping behavior before dinner or after dinner at hight sometime. He/she will make decision to spend much night time to turn on computer to click on share market website to research his/her share purchase choice to investigate whether his/her share price whether it rises up or falls down at the moment in order to make his/her share buying or selling decision at ever night time.

I mean the when the country has many people are share investors, their shares investment behavioral spenging time which will influence many shops lose customers at might often because the country will have many people feel need to spend night time to turn on computer or watch television to investigate share price variation.

So, the country will have many people / share investors choose to stay at home in order to carry on share price variation investigation behavior, they need to listen share market update news from radios or watch the share market update news from computer or TV at home every night. Consequenly, they must reduce times to leave themselves homes at night. So, their shopping behavior also will be reduced. Because these share investors feel need to spend time to investigate share price variation news at homes which can bring economic benefits (high opportunity benefits) when they choose to forgive to leave homes to go to shopping times (opportunity cost) every night.

On conclusion, it seems that when the country has many people are share investors, then their share price investigating behavior may bring negative shopping emotion at night. Consequently, the country's any one shop may lose many customers from this share investor consumer group in behavioral economic view. Hence, when the country's share investors number had been increasing rapidly, it will influence any shops lose many customers from this share investing customer group at night frequenly in short time, even long time in behavioral economic view, because their shopping desires or shopping emotion will be brought negative feeling when they make decisions to spend much time to listen radios or watch TV or computers share price update nes at night. Hence, share market will bring negative impact to influence consumer shopping desire or negative shopping emotion in behavioral economic view.

Can technology influence human shopping behavioral change?
Nowadays, technological development has reached mature stage, whether technological mature stage may bring positive or negative shopping emotion influence to global consumers. I shall aplly internet inventin or ecommerce shopping channel tool to explain whether internet technology can bring postive or negative influence to global consumer behavior in behavioral economic view.

Internet is a good technological tool, it brings e-commerce business chance. In fact, commonly, global has have many businessmen choose to use internet channel to carry on their products transactions between global online-buyers and their electronic websites. So, global many shoppers had begun to feel online shopping is more convenient to compare visiting shops shopping. Their shopping behaviors have been changed from internet technological tool. Global has many shoppers choose to buy any products from any overseas or local businessmen their web stores. They only need to spend time to find any businessmen their webstores to choose the most suitable products to pay visa to buy from their webstores. at homes. So, in general, global had have may shoppers had changed their shopping behaviors from visiting shops to visiting webstores at homes often.

So, it seems that internet technological tool had influenced global many shops disappear, but internet webstores will be replaced their actual shops on streets. Some of businessmen either they choose webstores to replace shops or choose websotes and shops both or still keep shops only. Hence, internet tool influences global businessmen have three kinds of products sale channels to let globa local and overseas consumers to choose how to buy their products. However, in fact, many of global shoppers, youngers and olders had begun to accept to buy any products from webstores. They feel to spend time to leave homes to visit shops , their shopping behaviors will be wasted time to not essential part to their daily lives. Hence, since internet technological invention, it had changed many consumers their traditional visiting shops shopping habit to change to buying products from webstores channel.

However, on the one hand, internet creates webstores ecommerce shopping channel to let global many consumers do not need to leave homes to go to shopping. It brings negative visiting shops shopping emotion to global general consumers nowadays. But on the other hand, it also brings positive visiting internet webstores shopping emotion to global general consumer nowadays. So, it seems that global many consumers feel that they often do not need to spend much time to go out shopping. Many global consumers feel convenient and enjoy to choose any products to buy from different internet webstores, when the online buyer chooses the most suitable product, he she only needs to pay visa card to buy the product from the online seller's webstore conveniently at home.

Hence, online shopping can bring economic benefit to online buyers, e.g. avoiding walking time or spending transport fare to visit the shop to go to shopping, shortening or reducing shopping time to do another important matter.

On conclusion, global many consumers began feel online shopping can bring more economic benefits on shortening shopping time, avoiding transport fare spending aspect. So, online shopping will be popular shopping behavior for future long time. It may encourage global many shoppers can make rapid shopping decision in short time in order to carry on any products buying transaction to global any one online shopper in short time easily in behavioral economic view. So, global many businessmen had begun to build themselves one attraction webstore in order to persuade different countries consumers to choose to click themselves webstores from internet channel to buy any kinds of products in short time easily.

So, internet technology had changed consumers traditional shopping behaviors to build positive online shopping emotion as well as raise online sellers' any products sale chance easily in behavioral economic view.

Why and how human behavior may influence the country's economic growth or recession?

When one country has many people choose to do the same matter for one period, whether their behavior may influence the country's pvera; economic growth or recession . I shall attempt to indicate cases toexplain their relationship as below:

For flowing rubblish behavioral case example, do you feel that when the country has many people often flow rubblish on the streets, instead of their flowing rubblish behavior may bring streets dirty? But, their flowing rubblish behavior may explain that this country has people may have enough money to buy food to ear, or enough cloths to wear, enough bottles of water to drink, even they may have enough money to buy new television, radio, refrigeraters , washing machines, desktops or laptops electronic home products from old to new to use in order to satisfy their living needs. So, when they flow old electronic home products, their flowing old home electronic products behaviors may seem that they have enough money to buy other new home electronic products to replace old home electronic products to use at homes.

However, it seems thaat this country ought have many people have jobs to do. So, many of them, they can easy to make purchase decison to flow any old home electronic products and buy any new home electronic products to use . Because this country has many people have jobs to do. So, they can often not use old home electonic products to become rubblishs to flow on streets after they had bought any kinds of new home electronic homes.

In fact, it also implies that this country's economy grows rapidly. So, many businesses can glow up rapdly. When they expanded their businesses, they must need to increase employees number in order to let they help themselves to raise productivity or serve their clients absolutely. So, when the country has many businesses can grow up, it seems that its economy must be better or it is improved to compare past. Due to many different kinds of home electronic products had been often bought to use by this country people in this period. So, this country's any streets can be observed that expensive electronic home products were flowed on streets anywhere. then, this country will have many electronic home products sellers can sell their home electronic products very easily. When this country has many people can find any kinds of jobs to do easily. So, due to unemploymen rate had been decreasing.

In behavioral economic view, as this many electronic home products rubblish country case, we can observe this country may have many people have jobs to do. So, consumption number has been increased long time. So, cheap food, or expensive home electronic products may be rubblish on any streets. This country's people , their flowing rubblish behaviors may be explained that many of people have enough jobs to do, so they have ability to buy any good taste food to eat or buy any kinds of expensive electronic home products to use. So, this country's economy may be improved for this long period. So, in behavioral economic view, when this country can have many electronic home products rubblishs are flowed on anywherer in streets frequently. It seems that this country will have many people have jobs to do, so it causes they often change old home electronic products or replaced them easily, when they have enough income to spend to buy any kinds of new home electronic products to use at homes easily. Moreover, their flowing old electronic home products behaviors also indicate that this country has many people their salaries may be increased in possible from their emplyers. When this country can have many different kinds of home electornic products are sold. It means that this country's electronic home products needs or demand had been increasing, due to many people have jobs to do and income increases to excite their living of needs also improve. Consequently, this country may seem have better economic improvement. We can observe from this country's electronic home products rubblish increasing income in theis period.

On conclusion, this country ought experience economic growth at this period. So, " flowing expensive electronic home rubblish increasing number " may seem that this country's economic growth is rapidly in this period, due to many people have jobs to do as well as salaries increase in this period.

Technology how impacts human behavior changing?

Technology how influences human behavior to bring changing? For example, online share purchase and sale transaction from smart phone brings share investor can do share buying or selling transation in any where and any time conveniently, non manual driving auto vehicle, bring car owner feels comfortable and spends free time to do other matter, e.g. reading, listening mucis in himself or herself car freely. electrical energy vehicle can help car owner to reduce air polluton and it can brings the drivers do not feel drive long time in any journeys in order to avoid air pollution for environmental protection responsible car drivers in our societies. Thus, they will drive long time in any journeys when they can drive electronic energy cars to replace oil energy cars.

However, online technology can also bring consumers can choose to stay at homes to buy any things from seller individual online webstore conveniently. Such as online technology can bring shoppers do not need to spend much time to visit shops to buy any things. They can choose any kinds of products from any online sellers individual online webstores conveniently at homes. Online technology excite busy consumers can make purchase decision easily as well as it can help online sellers sell any kinds of products from internet easily.

In behavioral economic view, technology can change human behavior to be improved, it can let human feels comfortable, more free time ro use, rapid making any decisions, such as apply smart phones to make share purchase or sale transaction decision, online shopping decision, even travelling any where decision in short time, when the traveller finds the most cheap hotel accommodation room price and air ticket price frm any travel agent online tourism webstore, then the potential travel customer can follow the online hotel accommodation price and air ticket price data to make decision when to buy the air ticket from the airline travel agent or make decision when to prebook which hotel accommodation room to go to the country to travel from online travel agent tourism webstores. So, technology can encourage global any country travelers to make anywhere to trvel rapidly. If the traveler can find the country's general hotel rooms and airline tickets prices had been decreasing more sightly. The traveler may make travel decision to choose the country to travel in short time, then he/she can prebook the country;s any hotel room and airline ticket to pay by visa fraom the country's any hotel and airline travel agent webstores., before one week, even one month or more easily. Hence, online technology can also encourage traveler individual frequent travel times to be increased, due to global travelers can find any hotel rooms and airline tickets prices from internet conveniently at homes. They do not need to spend time to visit any airline travel agent to enquire travel choice country's hotel rooms prices and airline ticket prices. They can compare global travel of countries choices ' all hotels rooms and airline agents air tickets prices to make prebook airline seat and hotel room decision before one week, one month even six months early.

On conclusion, online technology can encourage global travelers can make travelling any where and when traveling time desicions easily. It can excite tourism industry develops in long time. Also, such as electricity cars invention can encourage environment protection car owners do car purchase decision easily, because they can choose to drive electronic energy cars to replace oil energy cars in order to avoid air pollution occurs easily. So, electronic cars can increase electronic car purchasrs number, due to many of environmental protection attitude of car owners can choose to drive electricity cars to bring air cleans, even non -manual driving cars can encourage lazy driving and free time driving car owners to choose to buy non-manual (artificial intelligent) cars to drive , because they can spend much free time to read, listen music or do any matters in themselves cars, they do not need to drive cars, robotic (AI) auto driving machine is such one non-manual driver to help them to drive themselves cars confidently. So, non-manual driving cars can attract lazy and enjoying free time driving car owners to choose to buy to replace traditional manual cars to drive easily. Moreover, online share transaction can help any share investors to make share buying and selling decision in short time easily. When they can apply smart phones technological tool to carry on share buying and selling activities easily. They can observe any share rising or falling price suitation from smart phones in any where any any time easily. So, smart phone technology can help global any shareholders to make share purchase and sale transaction easily. So, technology can encourage human makes decision in short time rapidly.

How and why employees behaviors may influence economy development?

In behavioral economy view,I believe the country's any organizational employees behavior may bring indirect relationship to influence the country's long term economic development. I shall indicate past manufacture industry social development period to explain their relationship. For many countries' past business activities had belonged to manufacturing industry, such as US, UK past before 1980 year, it focused on steel manufacturing and steel manufacturing related machine products. So, US, Uk developed countries manufacturing industries may be past main country's economic income sources. I assume US , UK past had one million number different kinds of industries. They ought had about seven houndred thousand number organizational businesses were belonged to manufactured industry. They may include:
Steel manufacturing and steel related machine manufacturing, e.g. vehicle manufacturing, home appliances, e.g. washing machine, television, radio, refrigerate cooler, heater, air condition etc. different kinds of different kinds of steel -related manufacturing machine, they were manufactured from US, UK steel machine manufacturers. So, US, Uk the other three hundred thousand number industry may be general service industry, e.g. hotel service, restaurent, cinema, public transport service, tourism lesiure , wine bar, supermarket etc. different kinds of non-manufacturing industries business organizations were operated in UK, US past before 1980 year.
So, in UK, US developed countries industry development history, they ought have high percentage of businesses belonged to steel related manufacturing machine and steel products. Also, in the past before 1980 year, US, Uk business employers , they employed many workers are manufacturing workers. They needed to spend long time to work in factories. They were skillful workers, and they are trained to manufacturing cars, washing machine, television, heater, etc. even steel itself different kinds of steel related products to

prepare to deliver to their shops to sell to US, Uk local or overseas clients.

So, I believe that past UK, US ought employ many employees, they belonged to skillful manufacturing workers, manufacture increasing steel machine or steel related machine number of products rapidly daily. So, if UK, US had had many of these manufacturing factories owned high skillful workers, then their manufacturing steel-related machine or steel both kinds of products number must be influenced to raise rapidly. Consequently, their steel machine manufacturing products would been exported to overseas or would been sold to local both markets , they may be influenced to raise sale number. They (these manufacturing workers) needed to be trained to know how to manufactur these different kinds of machine products in the efficient teams and they ought to be trained to raise their efficiencies in order to shorten time to manufacturing many kinds of steel related manufacturing machine or steel itself products rapidly. So , if their efficiencies and manufacturing performance was improved, these US, UK any one manufacturing worker and their teams ought achieve raising productivities significantly.

Hence, when past UK, US manufacturing industry development period, if these two countries' any manufacturing factories could have many manufacturing workers could be trained to be skillful and proficient manufacturing workers. Then, in past every day to these factories workers, they ought help their steel or steel related manufacturing employers to raise any kinds of machine or steel products number in every team. So, when past in the manufacturing industry development, US, UK could have many factories' manufacturing workers themselves steel or steel related machine products manufacturing skill could be trained to to improve to any kinds of these machine or steel manufacuring products quality as well as their products number could be influenced to raise by themselves skillful improvement significantly every day.

Then, what would be influenced to occur to past UK, US manufacturing industry period? In behavioral economic view, when these two manufacturing industry developed countries, such as UK, US , if they had many factories workers can be trained to improve their skill in order to achieve any kinds of steel or steel-related machine products quality could be improved as well as products manufacturing number could be also increased absolutely. In consequence, past UK and US both countries ought increase themselves any kinds of steel and steel related machine products number to be supplied to themselves local shops to let local clients to choose any one kind of machine manufacturing products to buy easily as well as they could also export to supply overseas any countries to buy their different kinds of steel or steel related machine products to let overseas steel or steel related manufacturing machine product buyers, they can have many of these different kinds of these steel or steel-related different kinds of manufacturing machine from UK and UK these both countries easily to compare other countries.

On conclusion, I believe that past US, and UK macro manufacturing industry income GDP would increase significantly. So, they would have good economic growth performance because when many of these manufacturing workers themselves manufacturing effort could be improved. So, it explained when employees manufacturing abilities can influence economic growth indirectly.

Robots invention whether they can help organizations to raise efficiencies or inefficiencies?

In behavioral economic view, in any organizations, when the organization hopes its worker teams can raise efficiencies , the organization may choose to increase more workers number and/or it can provide training to improve these workets themselves skills in order to raise their efficiencies. For one warehouse example, when the warehouse increases many goods , they are needed to delivered these goods from the shelves to the delivering destination locations. If this warehouse supervisors feel these workers themselves goods delivery speeds are slow, which is possible due to this warehouse's workers number is not enough. So, this warehouse supervisor ought increase workers number in order to increase their goods delivery speed in order to deliver goods from the shelves to every indicated goods delivery destination in order to let any one lorry driver can transport the right kinds of goods and ensure the accurate goods number to transport to any one client home rapidly. However, if this warehouse supervisor planed to buy several warehouse goods delivery robots to assist these warehouse workers to find the right kinds of goods from shelves and then deliver to the right destination location in the warehouse. So, these warehouse orkers can concentrate on counting the accurate goods number and ensuring the right kinds of goods in order to prepare to let lorry drivers to transport these goods to these goods of buyers themselvers homes rapidly. Consequently, in the first step, robots can concentrate on finding th right goods from shelves and delivers them to the right goods transportation of location destination. Then, in the second step, these warehouse workers can concentrate on counting the accurate goods number and ensuring the right kinds of goods in order to prepare to put them to the lorry. Consequently, when warehouse robots and warehouse workers can cooperate to work together, the most important, robots, can deal on finding the right kinds of goods and deal on delivering the accurate number of goods of job duty as well as these warehouse workers can only concentrte on counting the right kinds of goods number in order to avoid it has none any mistake of wrong kinds of goods and inaccurate goods of delivery number to be transported to the lorry and to deliver to any one buyer's home.

So, it seems that warehouse robots ought help any one warehouse worker to raise himself efficiency and avoid goods delivery of mistake occurrence easily as well as their help to warehouse workers that can let any one goods buyer feels their goods can be delivered to their homes rapidly. Moreover, warehouse robots can also help these warehouse workers to raise efficiencies because warehouse robots can help them to shorten goods delivery time between any one shelf and any one goods delivery destination of location in the warehuse because robots may help them to find the right kinds of goods from the right shelf in the short time. So, any one worker does not need to spend long time to seek anywhere is the right shelf location for the kind of goods when the kind of goods are needed to deliver to the buyer's home from lorry. Warehouse robots can help them to do this aspect of " finding the goods from the right shelf in short time job duty". So, any one warehouse worker only needed tospend less time to do the counting of any right kind of goods number and ensuring the right kind of goods job duty. Consequently, this warehouse 's any one worker, his any one kind of goods delivery time may be reduced, because robots' assistance and they may have more confidence to avoid mistake to deliver the wrong number of goods and/or the wrong kind of goods to any one goods buyer's home.

On conclusion, it seems that warehouse robots ought may help any one warehouse worker to raise efficiency for any one team in the warehouse as well as the warehouse any one supervisor does not need to spend much time to observe any one worker individual performance for " goods delivery job duty aspect" because their goods delivery job duty that had been replaced to do by these several warehouse robots. Robots can achieve the more accurate of right kinds of goods and the right number of goods delviery job performance to compare any one of human warehouse worker themselves right kinds of goods of delivery and right number of goods of delivery job performance. So, when robots can participate to cooperate with this warehouse's any one worker to do their goods of delivery job duty in this warehouse every day. Then, robots can raies any one of supervisor individual confidence in order to let they do not need to spend time to observe any one of worker individual whose goods of delivery job performane. They can concentrate on supervising any one worker whose goods transport to lorry in the final step in order to avoid to deliver wrong goods number and / or wrong kind of goods to any one goods buyer's home every day. Consequently, this warehouse's overall teams of their delviery of goods performance many be improved by robotss' participatin to goods of delivery task as well as this warehouse's oveall teams themselves efficiencies may be influenced to raise by robots' goods of delivery task participation.

Why social behavior may influence organizational strategy needs to be changed ?

Why any organizations need to know whether nowadays social behaivor how has been changing in order to implement the kind of the most right strategy to achieve the profit aim pursue in possible. I shall indicate nowadays ecommerce or online, customer shopping behavior to explain above question concerns they ought have close relationship between social behavior and organizational strategic choice or organizational behavioral changing need.

On nowadays ecommerce business, or online shopping model, this kind of shopping model in global many young and old age consumers like to apply internet tool to choose any country sellers website stores in order to stay at home to buy any kinds of products from themselves webstores in global societies.

In fact, online shopping model had been popular for long time above to twenty years. Most of global sellers will make decision to design themselves webstores in order to attract global many online buyers to choose to buy their products from themselves webstores. So, it seems that social consumers purchase behaviors had been changed to online shopping from internet invention.

Hence, social consumers purchase behavioral changes may influence any organizations' strategies need to be changed from visiting shops purchase strategy model to online purchase strategy model, if the seller still concentrate on concentrate on considerate how to design itelf , but neglects to considerate how to design itself webstore, e.g. how to design attract product photos to put on itself webstore, how to arrange sale price information location to be putted on webstore and visa card payment location on itself webstore in order to let any one online buyer can feel very easier to buy itself any kinds of products from itself webstore. Then, its potential online buyers will be influenced to increase number when they can find this online seller itself any kinds of products photes and every kinds of product sale price information and visa card payment channel locations easily from itself webstore.

So, it implies that nowadays any one seller ought need to design one webstore to let any one online overseas and domestic consumers can have chance to click itself webstore to choose any one kind of product to buy conveniently when he/she does not hope to leave him/her home to go to shop, because nowadays social shopping behaviors had been influenced to change when internet invention, them it gives another online purchase method to replace visiting shops purchase method to global any one buyer in nowadays societies.

So, if nowadays any one seller still concentrate on how to design itself shop display in order to put any kinds of product on shelf in order to let any one visiting shop customer to find the kind of product to buy, but it neglects to change to choose to pursue another new technological shopping method, such as webstore purchase method in order to implement effective strategy to design the most right webstore as well as in order to attract global overseas and local consumers to find itself webstore easily from website and find its any one kind of product phots and sale price and visa card payment button in order to choose to buy itself any kinds of products in the short time. Consequently I believe that the seller will lose many customers from overseas and local when its other same or similar product sellers choose to design themselves webstores in order to let global any one product buyer can buy themselves any one kind of product when they can pay visa card to buy their products from them webstores conveniently when they stay at home habitly. Then, the seller will lose many global potential customers in long time.

On conclusion, in behavioral economic view, any consumer behavioral social changing, which will influence any in order to avoid customers number loses significantly . In future time, organizations need to make rapid decision in order to implement the most reasonable and the most useful strategy in order to avoid global potential customers number reduces or lose them in long time. So, social behavioral changing environment ought influence any global organizations need to decide how to change themselves strategies in order to avoid customers loses significantly in future time.

How and why human behavior may influence economic growth or recession?

May ourselves daily behaviors influence our global societial continue economic growth or recession? Do they have cause and effect close relationship between human behaviors and global economic growth or recession? I shall apply behavioral economic theory to analyze and explain whether ourselves daily behaviors and our global societial economic growth or recession which have close cause and effect relationship as below:

Every country itself economic development must depend on any business activities, otherwise, any kinds of business activities must need ourselves business activities or behaviors in order to achieve any business activities as well as achieve the country's overall economic development in macro view.

However, any country's overall business activites or behaviors which must depend on any kinds of individual businessmen, themselves employees daily working behavior or activity or performance in order to help them to attract or increase many clients number to acieve " earning profit" aim. So, it seems that any individual business, itself overall every department individual working behavior is one main factor to influence the company's overall business performance.

For agricultural fruit and meat food farming industry example, such as New Zealand is a farming main target industry country. It had had many New Zealanders were daily themselves own farming businesses for many years. Their farming businesses include growing fruit, sheep, cow, pig pork, meat etc. food sale business. If the New Zealand farmer owned a large size farming land, then he will choose either growing fruit or feeding sheeps, pigs, cows to be meat to to transport to New Zealand supermarkets to help them to sell to their farmers meet to New Zealanders in order to earn profit. Thus, if the New Zealand farmer owned large size of farming lands, then he needs to employ many farming employees (farming workers) to help him to carry on farming business daily tasks, e.g. picking up friuts, feeding pigs, cows, sheeps to eat food daily. These daily farming jobs are very important to influence this New Zealand farmer's meats or fruits sale number whether they can be easy or diffcult to sell in New Zealand supermarkets , if these farming workers can own encough farming knowledge or skill to know how to pick up fruits method and make judgement to know whether it is right time to pick up the kind of fruits from the trees , as well as know how feed this pigs, sheeps, cows to eat food in order to let they are better health. Consequently, their farming behaviors which can let these animals can provide the best taste and enough meat from these animals to let New Zealander to buy to eat from New Zealand any one supermarket. Even these New Zealand farming workers can know whether the kinds of fruits, e.g. oranges, apples, gapes etc. fruits whether they ought be picked up from the trees at the right time. Consequently, they can make judgement to decide to pick up any kinds of the best taste fruits to let any one New Zealander to buy to eat from any one supermarket in New Zealand. Otherwise, if they do not make judegement to know whether the kind of fruit ought not be picked up because they still need longer time to continue grow up to increase fruit size and better taste from the trees in order to let any one fruit buyer can feel better taste when they eat this kind of fruit later. If they can buy this kind of fruit to eat later, then this New Zealand farmer's his fruit buyers can buy the best taste of this kind of fruit to eat from an yone supermarket in New Zealand. Consequently, many New Zealand supermarkets will choose to buy any kinds of fruits from this farmer fruit supplier when they feel this farmer's fruits can provide more better taste fruits to compare other farmers' fruits.

Thus, due to New Zealand is one farming main income source country. It's any kinds of fruits and meats need to be export to overseas to sell , instead of local sale. It's GDP percent is very high to whole country 's overall income source. So, any one New Zealand farmer individual and any one farming worker individual working behavior will influence its economy whether it is influenced to grow or recession possible. Moreover, it also seems that farming workers' farming knowledge and skill will influence themselves farming daily activities to achieve the aim of the number of increase or decrease to any kinds of fruits whether they are better taste or the number of increase of decrease to any kinds of meats whether they are better taste to supply to any one New Zealand fruit or meat buyers to eat from any one New Zealand supermarket. So, it implies that any one New Zealand farming worker individual farming behavior may influence any kinds of fruits or any kinds of meat taste because they are transported to any one supermarket to sell in New Zealand.

Consequently, if New Zealans had many farmers can teach god farming knowledge and skill to let their any one farming workers know how to decide judgement to decide when it is right time to pick up any kinds of fruits from trees , or how to grow them on soil in order to let they can grow rapidly. Then, many different kinds of fruits can be provided to let any one New Zealanders can eat the best taste of fruits when their fruits are supplied to any one New Zealand supermarkets. Even, if they knew how to feed foods to pigs, cows, sheeps to eat daily. Then they can be more health and they can provide the best taste of meats to let any one New Zealanders can buy their meats from any one New Zealand supermarkets. Moreover, their fruits and meats can be transported to overseas to let any one country fruits or meats buyers can choose any kinds of New Zealand meats and fruits to buy to eat from themselves countries supermarkets. Then, many overseas fruit and meat buyers will perfer to choose New Zealand any kinds of fruits or meats to buy to compare other countries fruits or meats to buy when they go to any one local supermarkets.

On conclusion, it seems that New Zealand farming workers themselves farming behavior may influence their farming employers any kinds of fruits or meats sale number and income because their farming task behaviors must influence whether their fruits or meats taste are the better taste or worse taste to compare their other local farmers (the farmer competitors) whose fruits or meats taste. If tthe farmer's any one farming worker can be trained to learn how to know to feed animals skill and when is the most right time to pick up any kinds of fruits from trees or how to grow them on the soil methods. Due to these farming worker individual farming behavior may influence his different finds of fruits and meats sale number to be increase or decrease, so these any one New Zealand farmer must need to depend on any one farming worker whose farming working methods, if their farming working behaviors can be the best to influence any kinds of fruits to grow rapid or any kinds of pigs, cows, sheeps animals grow up rapidly , then their sale number may be increase significantly and their taste can be improved to let any New Zealand or overseas meat or fruit buyer to buy to eat to feel from any one New Zealand or overseas supermarkets, then New Zealand's agriculture industry must be influenced to increase. In the world, any one fruit or meat buyer must choose to buy New Zealand's fruit and meat to eat in prefer to compare other countries' fruits and meats. So, New Zealand's GDP may be influenced to raise from any one New Zealand farming worker individual farming working behaviors.

Reasons why human behavior may influence economic recession or growth?

Can ourselves daily behaviors or activies influence ourselves countries' economic growth or recession? I shall attempt to explain the reasons why they have direct or indirect relationship between human behavior and economy growth or recession as below:

I shall indicate environment pollution case to attempt to explain above question. Our societies had been experiencing servious environment pollution challenge. However, environment pollution , such as air pollution is caused by air planes and vehicles emission by air planes and vehicles emission as well as water pollution is caused by plastic rubblish, or dirty water or oil or gas chemical material, these both kinds of pollution ought may bring economic recession and this both kinds of pollution are caused by human ourselves daily foolish activities.

I believe human behavior and economy and pollution which have cause and effect relationship. I shall analyze this environment pollution case to explain why they have case and effect relationship between human foolish behavior and environment pollution and economic recession as below:

When global societies had many people like to buy cars to drive to bring emission to fresh air on the roads as well as many manufacturing factories will bring emission to pollute fresh air in their manufacturing processes. Factories and cars will bring air pollution , due to factories need to pollute fresh air in order to manufacture many products and car owners need to drive their cars to go to offices or leisure places. Their cars will also bring emisson to pollute fresh air. On consequence, car owners themselves frequent driving behaviors and factory workers themselves frequent manufacturing behaviors may bring environment pollution. Technology or human behavior whether may influence economic growth or recession. Moreover, air planes also brings emission to pollute air when they are flying in sky. Also, when ships bring oil pollution or sea plastic rubblishs bring pollution to global oceans.

In fact, manufactuers and cars owners, such as factories workers manufacturing behaviours ans car owners driving behaviors and pilots driving air planes flying behaviors and ships transport behaviors, which may cause plastic rubblish, oil or gas emission to sky or sea or on the road to cause ocean and air pollution is serious. However, human ourselves need to buy cars to drive to satisfy ourselves driving leisure or enjoyment, travelers need to catch air planes to travel to enjoy leisure needs, factories workers need help factories to manufacture many products to sell to customers to satisfy their using needs. oil exploration needs to find lands to explore new oil lands.

All of these business and leisure activites may bring serious air and water pollution. However, due to serious air and water pollution will bring earth warming challenge , such as some countries temperature will be influences to rise up to 40 degree or higher br earth warming. However, earth warming is caused by air and ocean pollution. Pollution must be caused by human ourselves, driving cars leisure and factories manufacturing business activities. Hence, if human decided to continue to do these foolish behaviors, we only pursue to manufacture different kinds of industrial products or drive cars to enjoy leisure aims, but we also neglect ourselves behaviors may bring environment pollution. Then, earth warming or earth temperature will be influenced to rise up absolutely in long term. Moreover, if our future earth will be influenced to bring serious high temperature effect by human ourselves these foolish behaviors.

On consequencey, warth warming will bring serious economic losses in possible because when ourselves earth temperature had been influenced to rise up to 40 degree or high. Ourselves health will be caused poor, due to we will feel difficult breath, we must need often tried and hard to work, due to our nervous and health will be influenced to poor by pollution and earth warming effect. Also, we need to pay more money to see doctors when we had long life. Then, our societies will lose may strong labors to help manufacturers to work, e.g. factories will reduce workers number to help manufacturers to produce more different kinds of products, due to workers health is general poor. Due to lacking enough workers to manufacture products, our societies will begin to reduce enough supply number of products to sell to global consumers to satisfy their use needs.

On conclusion, in behaviroal economic view, our societies will lose many labors due to their bodies are not health by air and water pollution. Global economic and business activities will be influenced to worse by global workers reducing number reason. So, economic recession will begin to occur in possible when pollution reaches the serious level.

CHAPTER FIVE

Robots Sale And Manufacture Market Development

Which kinds of industries will be
influenced by future (AI)
technological development?

What (AI) technological development will influence what kinds of UK and US industries development within ten years? Are environment and education and automatic manufacturing technologies will be UK and US future (AI) new technological development trends? What will be the difference between the (AI) developed countries and (non AI) developing countries future technologies development both in the future?

1 (AI) online teaching technology development
Future, (AI) online teaching method will be popular to be applied to teach to any university in possible, even secondary and primary schools. Because internet service is free charge to any students in any countries. Many different age students who can know how to apply internet as well as internet studying is very convenient to any students who can to internet to learn or study in home or public library or school library conveniently. Teachers do not need spend much time to teach students in classroom. They can use internet to teach teachers by face to face seeing and talking to their individual

student from every student's computer. So, students do not also often spend much time to go to school to learn. So, developing any fast speed and time saving and talking and listening online teaching methods will be popular needs to any UK primary and secondary and university students in the future. It will be one new technological teaching method to change the traditional classroom educational method in UK and schools. For example, when one UK student who had left UK and is living in another country long time. If any UK school did not provide online teaching service to any UK students. It means that the UK citizen can not choose study himself/herself any UK school if who still hope to study any UK course when who is living in another country. Even one foreign student who does not go to UK to study, if he/she can find any UK primary or secondary or university to study from online. Then, the UK school won't lose one foreign student, due to it does not provide online teaching method to any foreign students. So, online Technology educational learning method will be one popular learning method which is enhanced, supported, mediated or assessed by the use of electronic media. Technology also enhanced learning may involve the use of new or established technology and/or the creation of new learning material. It may be deployed both locally and at a distance (i.e. a combination of traditional and e-learning approaches), to learning that is delivered entirely online. Online learning technology characteristics (features) include identification of a project lead for each area of any learning strategy, identification of two " quick win" for example lecture capture, electronic submission and feedback.

How can online technology enhance learning at UK any schools? It will include these several aspects to analyze. On identifying, prioritizing and innovation hand, online technology is a process for resourcing, prioritizing, acquiring and evaluating school software and hardware for UK any school needs. On staff development learning plan and a student skills development plan hand, UK schools need to establish a base-line policy on the standard (minimum) technology enhanced learning expectation for education each program and module and a mechanism for updating the schools' policies. On evaluation and research hand, a mechanism for engaging the owners of the technology enhanced learning strategy with best practice in the sector including contributing to and benefiting from pedagogical research and the evaluation of the student experience to UK any school.

Thus, UK schools can apply (AI) teachers to teach their students from online technological teaching channel to develop on educational aspect, such as (AI) teachers' digital literacies and appropriate technical skills that equip UK students for life-long learning, graduate level employment and professional practice, be empowered to learn how to learn with online teaching technology, using online technology to engage in interactive, creative and co-constructed learning with the potential for online learning in an interdisciplinary and international context, using online teaching technology to engage in learning with and from people from anywhere in the world, be supported on placement and in workplace learning through mobile applications and other supportive technologies that facilitate their online learning when away from the classroom, having access to innovative methods of online learning teaching and assessment that are the foundation of a research-lead academic environment, engaging with UK schools in developing , implementing and reviewing the technology enhanced learning strategy. Thus, in the future, it is important to build a capacity to apply (AI) teaching robots to teach their students from the online education technology to adopt future learning innovation and student individual online learning need (demand) to UK any school (AI) robotic online teaching trend.

There are many examples where UK academics working in isolation or in small UK teaching organizations or classroom learning groups have developed (AI) robotic teaching innovation that have a positive impact on UK students' academic experience , but these have remained isolated to particular modules or occasionally program. The aim of education researching online learning process is to identify the good (AI) robotic teachers' online teaching innovation that is being developed and to prioritize those that have the potential to make a significant contribution to improving the academic student experience at UK any schools. This online teaching process will need any UK schools which can plan how to apply limited resources necessary to achieve online teaching. In addition, the online teaching research process would evaluate and prioritize large scale educational software and hardware requests for primary, secondary and university students' requests. An important part to this process will be to ensure the integration of (AI) robotic teaching tools and their educational method to be applied to online educational products and packages that school staff and students regular use to make routine working and access as seamless as possible.

Decisions about school administrative online technologies should not be taken in isolation before assessing the impact on UK teaching staff. In addition, a range of techniques such as, (AI) robotic online expert facilitation, (AI) robotic coaching and peer support will be used to support individuals, groups or longer academic units, who are learning on major technology enhanced (AI) robotic teching online learning projects. Staff engagement may also facilitated through incorporating technology that is used in teaching staff research and/or professional activity that can be cooperated into their teaching.

Consequently, (AI) robotic online learning technology can develop UK students skills, UK schools need to understand how UK students understand technology and learn with it, therefore the digital literacy strategy needs to be considered as part of the overall strategy as well as the relevant skills development in UK employability strategy. So, in the future, (AI) teaching robotic online learning and teaching technology will make it clear that students will develop technical skills the appropriate level for graduate employability and professional practice. Also, in the future, the (AI) robotic teaching online technology can enhance learning working group to discuss external development, that are of educational strategic importance, understanding and evaluating current best practice and research and understanding and evaluating the online educational strategic contribution that pedagogical research and student feedback can have on online educational strategy, policy and practice. The (AI) robotic teaching e-learning unit is responsible for informing and educating. This could be done by, for example, providing a short digest of relevant information for each meeting and by setting aside a proportion of each school meeting to discuss a topic of particular (AI) robotic teachers to be applied to online educational strategic interest to every school. Academics that have not got a specialist interest in (AI) robotic teaching online educational technology enhanced learning will need relevant information at an appropriate time. This could be provided at a school department or faculty level and this will have clear links to the staff and (AI) robotic teaching online teaching development plan. Hence, future (AI) robotic teaching online educational development strategy will influence any UK or US educational school technological improvement in the future (AI) robotic online teaching method.

2 (AI) robotic environmental protection technology

Can future (AI) robotic environment technology be valid to human to develop? Nowadays, global air and water pollution is serious. For example, UK has many farming is polluted by the water and air pollution. It will influence UK farmers' income if whose farm land (natural resource) is polluted by water or air (natural resource). Even it will influence UK citizen will encounter food shortage if UK farmers can not grow any fresh and health food to provide the enough food numbers to eat every day. Moreover, air and water pollution will influence UK citizen drink the polluted water and breathe the dirty air to live every day. This natural resource (air and water challenge) will influence UK citizen health to cause illness , even death every easily. So, UK government can not neglect the natural environment pollution challenge. The environmental protection technology will help the UK and development countries to solve the challenge of climate change to avoid or reduce farming, foods, or vegetable or fruits or rice, pork, livestock numbers loss threats, i.e. the development and deployment of low carbon energy technology, including technology for the efficient use of energy. The commercialization of low carbon energy and energy efficiency technologies in the UK, with a specific focus on the demonstration and deployment phases of bringing low carbon technologies to UK market.

The UK Government needs to deliver a low carbon economy and to meet UK ambitions emission reduction target. So, low carbon and environmental protection technology researching and development will reduce the carbon intensity of energy production as well as reduce energy demand, towards meeting the contributing UK's ambitions production as well as reduce energy demand, and renewable energy goals. The use of energy (including transportation fuel) and the UK's targets on climate change, for example, by helping the UK make a step change in increasing deployment of renewable energy, improving UK energy efficiency and helping low carbon technologies reach the market. The development of low carbon technologies, and to realize the benefits of doing so in terms ensuring security of energy supply for the UK future economy development.

In UK, private sector investment in technology innovation in the low carbon energy sector will other sectors of the economy. So, in UK energy technologies are likely needed to be developed to avoid dangerous climate change, or an acceptable cost. So, in the future, UK government will need to consider to research environment protection and low carbon energy technology. The activities will reduce carbon emissions, or have the potential to reduce carbon emissions on the longer term, through the use of energy technology will accelerate development and deployment of low-carbon energy and energy efficiency technologies will capacity in the demonstration and deployment of low carbon technologies. Innovation in the energy sector is the only way to identify, develop and reduce the costs of new and improved technologies for the extractions, generation, distribution and use of energy. It has long been an important means of achieving the UK's energy policy aims of a secure and affordable energy supply, as well as to develop the environmentally friendly technologies that are required in UK response to climate change, i.e. nuclear, wind or water, sun energy technology, which is future new energy technology is suitable to research to create to apply instead of current electricity energy.

How global warming influences UK agriculture growth. Scientists have also been fighting the use of chlorine in municipal water systems to kill various strands of bacteria. Chlorine reduces by about 80% the number of alimentary tract diseases relative to polluted, unchlorinated water. A relatively new genetically modified agricultural products. They were partly successful in Europe, such as UK (some countries banned genetically modified products) in spite of the fact that neither history nor research supports their case. People began to modify plants as early as the beginning of the agricultural revolution (8000 to 10,000 years ago), when they started seed selection and who have continued ever since. The green revolution of the 1960 year brought about strains of grans and rice more resistant to a variety of local conditions. The effects have been that countries like India, which had suffered from recurrent famines over the millennia, became self-sufficient in food due to the resultant sharp increase in agricultural productivity. It was a real science and technology over the poverty dominating most of human history. But it is precisely the products of science and technology that ecologists are so deathly afraid of. In an interesting study in a quarter (28%) of clinically analyzed cases of obsessive compulsive disorder were cases resulting from the fear of global warming.

To destroy the modern, whether industrial or postindustrial, civilization, human have to destroy an important engine of economic growth, that is its energy sources. And this is what eco-warriors try to achieve under the banner of against global warming. Thus, UK government will have responsibility to attempt to research new technology to fight global warming challenge for itself farmer benefits and even global benefits both on the future.

Hence, future (AI) robotic development can be applied to

environment protection aspect. Future (AI) robotic tools can help human to predict when and how any why environment pollution will occur in which countries and (AI) robotic tools can be one environment protection machine to gather environment pollution information to give opinions to human how we ought need to do in anywhere in order to avoid the places' environment pollution will become serious in influence our health. So, future (AI) robotic machince will be one predictive environmental pollution and bad climate change machine and it can give opinions to avoid serious environment pollution and give solutions to solve environment pollution any country.

(AI) will give global warming technological protection economic influence opinion to human

Some future economists indicated reasons to explain why UK government and businessmen needed to consider how to develop natural environment protection technology to avoid global warming challenge to influence UK economy development. They indicated the anthropogenic (human-made) global warming resulting from the increase in "greenhouse gas". They offered their perspectives on the scientific valid of anthropogenic global warming phenomenon, its probability of occur and expected consequences and is dominated by technologists, economists and political scientists, who considered the need to make the horribly costly adjustments in energy generation and usage suggested by climate alarmists.

Many stress that global warming is primarily caused by other phenomena than human use of fossil fuels or human activities in general. They are looking at the activities of the sun and impact of the larger universe as the main source of global warming and stress that global warmings (plural) happen intermittently with global cooling. I shall explain why global climate warming will influence to the political and economics of the issue to UK country. For it is the latter, rather than the global warming itself, that will pose a challenge to the Western world, such as UK and the world at large in the future. Scientists concerned who should move forward with policy measures to avert the alleged disaster. They also apply manufacturing theories to support enough to frighten politicians into action and scare societies into acceptance of measures that would sharply reduce UK citizen their living standards. Otherwise, UK politicians had support that bureaucracies were established, money allocated and lobbies created dependent on the new kind of subsidies. In consequences, climate alarmism and resultant interventions in national economies and human activities have become the increasingly wide spread and increasingly cost reality. With the growing availability of money distributed, and even more promised, a range of benefit of the global warming machinery has been on the increase. So, if UK government did not concern how to innovate new weather protection technology to avoid climate change adverse (poor) influence. It is possible that billions of dollars of UK public money are needed to spend on research global warming challenge because global warming will influence UK agricultural industry. UK agricultural industry is one important export income source to raise UK GDP income every year. If global warming become very serious to influence UK weather to be bad to cause UK farmers who can not grow good taste food and vegetable to supply to domestic and overseas food consumers to eat. Then, UK will loss much GDP income from local agricultural export sale. It seems global warming and agricultural production which has direct relationship to influence UK economy development in the future.

The main problem with climatology is that it must be based as already stressed on very many variables affecting climate and too few hard data necessity. Differences apply not only with respect to the scale of changes obtained, but even to their direction (rising or declining temperature). Some weather scientists indicated to concern global warming challenge. In consequence, it would be impossible to discover if and where errors were made not only in estimating relationships between variables but also in the quality of data used. (Hauser, J. Tellis, G. J; Griffin, A. 2006) They were comparing average temperatures measured some 30, 40 or 50 years ago by, say, 90 % weather stations in the countryside and 10 %

stations in the cities with contemporary average temperatures measured by weather stations located today on 50:50 basis in the countryside and cities. Then, one could obtain the increasing temperatures without any real world climate or even weather changes. Comparability would be ensured if the same number of countryside-located and city-located weather stations had been compared for different periods. The alarmists intentionally mix up " temperature growth" with the trend of temperature growth. To give an example, if in the first decade the temperature grew by 0.5 % degree, in second decade it grew by 0.3 % and in third decade it grew by 0.1%, what was registered was a growth in the temperature, but certainly not a trend of growing temperature. A fourth decade should, on the basis of the trend, bring about no change in the temperature.

To conclude, scientists believed that global warming was caused by human's bad behavior more than natural environment influence. So, it is human's responsibility needs to solve this challenge, due to who feel earning profit aim is more important to protect natural environment, e.g. air and water pollution , due to manufacturing process is the main factor. So, UK has responsibility to attempt to research how to solve global warming challenge , such as it has many famous scientists who can devote their scientific skills to cooperate to solve global warming challenge with other countries' scientists. Some weather scientists also hypothesized that human may be at the end of the present warming period. If they are right, it would be bad for humanity, as warmer periods have always been associated with better conditions for economic activity. To sum up, scientists believed that global warming will influence human economic activity to be bad.

Future (AI) robotic environmental protection machine can give opinions to UK farmers:

Climate alarmists were able to convince a large part of the Western public and a majority of Western politicians of the cause of fighting against the global warming. It supposes itself in an instinctive preference for collectivist solutions in economic and social spheres, with negative to disastrous consequences when scientists are applied in practice, so UK government needs to concern global warming challenge, due to it is possible that it will influence UK natural environment weather to be poor to influence many UK farmers' agricultural and vegetable and fruit and rice wheat etc. food growth successfully. What is the global warming influence to cause disease? For example, ecological alarmists and activists (eco-warriors) never admit they are wrong, they long pursued their fear mongering campaign against chlorine. Their success in branding DDT a dangerous substance had a negative impact on the malaria eradication campaign in poorer parts of the world. Alternatives to be have been far less effective and the result has been the resurgence of malaria cases and the manifold increase in malaria -caused deaths to the largest extent in Africa.

3 (AI) robotic automation technology in manufacturing industry Future, (AI) robotic automation technology can be applied to manufacturing industry. For example, nowadays, UK computer and space explore technology had reached the mature stage. It means that UK government ought not need to continue spend much resource to research these two kind technologies. Otherwise, the (AI)robotic automatic manufacturing technology, e.g. human intelligence new product. It has need to develop because human intelligence machines will bring beneficial to satisfy human everyday life need, e.g. hospital patients' activities need, if the patent who can not walk easily, but the human intelligence machine can assist the patient walk to anywhere conveniently. So, he/she does not need to sit on wheel chair and apply the human intelligence machine man to help him/her to drive on the intelligence automatic driving vehicle to go to anywhere conveniently.

Otherwise, increased automation in low wage countries, e.g. China, Korea, Africa, Hong Kong etc. which have traditionally manufacturing firms, could use automatic technological manufacturing to bring lose cost advantage and potentially lose their ability of achieving rapid economy growth by shifting workers to factory jobs. So, UK government and businessmen needs to consider automation technology development, i.e. 3D printing manufacturing industry will encourage UK companies to move manufacturing process, closer to gain the biggest advantage from this 3D automation technology development.

A growing concern of premature de-industrialization in energy and developing countries could require new models and a need un-skillful the UK workforce. In the future, the best way toward for UK cities will reduce their exposure to automation is to boost their technological dynamic and attract more UK skilled workers. Automation technology progress can give UK manufacturers' employee benefits, such as long term healthy productivity improvement, raising productivity efficiency and product quality, macroeconomic and microeconomic effects of automation technological change, it's change will be beneficial to UK society, i.e. automation active labor market policies, which could help UK job seekers find jobs from training to incentive to support self-employment to create high technological job employment chance in UK society. So, raising science, technology, engineering and math subjects update skills level are needed to UK any universities, which can be increasingly important in UK society, these factors could complicate the ability of UK high automation technology education to adopt to the UK automation manufacturing technological change. A talent mismatch already exists in UK, with many well UK educated workers can find employment in lower-skilled jobs. To combat this, greater coordination will be needed between the education, training and employment sectors in UK society.

Why are high automatic technology product development models needed to research to UK any manufacturers? UK government and manufacturers need to consider how to achieve high technology product development models. According to Hauser et al. (2006) indicated the high technology (high tech.) development process, is influenced by the innovative process, bringing products on exception value which stimulate product market demand. Innovation provides products the specific basis for which world economies compete with each other on the global market. Able to find new solutions, innovations generate significant changes in existing markets, destroy them, or create new marketing (Hauser et al. 2006). So, UK manufacturers need to concern on any manufacturing high technology product development process because which can influence any new products development to manufacture to sell to any overseas or domestic both markets successfully.

What is high tech. product meaning? Mohr et al. (2010) argues that there are two reasons why it is important to clarify and specific high technology : (1) due to the impact of technologies on the economy, attempts are made to classify economic production and incomes ; (2) due to the impact of high tech. on the environment. Standard marketing strategies are being modified and adopted , therefore, it is necessary to know the products to focus on. Why UK manufacturers need to consider high technological product process. Nowadays, high tech. products are complex, advanced, requiring specific technical knowledge, which is technologically not discontinued and being produced at the companies which have twice as many technical personnel and invest twice as many in scientific research and development than other companies. Moreover, these products are time-sensitive as scientists are continuously searching for new approaches for invention of more advanced technologies which make all preceding ones lower-ranking. The most important, nowadays global consumers will adopt the particular technology. It means that global customers may delay adopting new high-tech. products and in order to mitigate the prolonged uncertainty require a high degree of education and information about the product and need post-purchase reassurance. Anyway, nowadays customer individual needs in high tech. environments are characterized by sudden changes related to unpredictable fashion. Even, consumers concern about how to preserve new product' competitive technological standard is completely incompatible with technological uncertainty. The most important factor is the prevalence rate of any new products development process, which is influenced by slower than of traditional products. In many cases high-tech. automatic product market are being materialized slower than which are expected. The technological uncertainty challenges will exist in development process, such as uncertainty related to the timetable for development of the question whether the new product will be function as promised. In automatic high-tech. industries, the time requires for product development is difficult to predict as , commonly, it takes longer than expected , uncertainty related to unanticipated consequences and uncertainty about the product life cycle related to competition products. In conclusion, these factors will influence new automatic technology product development process unsuccessful, so UK manufacturers will need to concern on any high technological automatic product's manufacturing process.

Future economists predict automatic technology how to influence future UK economy

Before, all over the world presented picture of demonstrate in London on the occasion of the meeting of the G20. Some economists indicated disastrous economy consequences will occur to any one of Western country , such as UK, so if any one of Western country did not consider automatic technology development to itself country. They indicated one example, such as material incentives to produce disappeared throughout Russia and, when Society leadership called off the experiment, the country faced industrial output reduced to 10% of what had been registered in 1914 and agricultural output reduced to such low levels as to cause widespread famine.

Why would UK encounter disastrous economy consequences if UK government did not encourage manufacturers spend money to invest to innovate automatic technology industry? According to a variety of anthropological studies, a collectivity is unable to operate efficiently with everybody giving talent workers have chance to devote whose best effort to manufacture any high technological products, e.g. human intelligence vehicle or airplane. Hence, economic incentives are needed to UK manufacturers to invest high technological automatic industry development. Because the economists predict UK will have many talent worker numbers, their number will be more than a certain number of normal effort workers, due to UK technological education level is very excellent to provide to train many young technological manufacturing students to find this kind of high technological manufacturing job. So, the high technological manufacturing job seekers will increase and it won't decrease to UK job market in the future.

Assuming that UK high technological automatic manufacturing workers who would desire only to introduce changes in the workings of the international economic order and policies of countries participating in the present economic order rather than change the order itself, what will be UK manufacturers their specific economic preferences in the future? It implies tnat either concentrate on spending more investment to automatic high technological development, e.g. human intelligence automatic high technological products or still concentrate on spending more investment to common traditional technological products.

However, UK was a developed Western country which had had strong automatic high technological development effort very long time. Otherwise, it compared to some developing countries, such as Asian China, Hong Kong, Korea etc. Asian countries their future economic growth rate will show un- surprising , different patterns, so the Asian countries has weak effort to invest high automatic technological product development, such as human intelligence technological development. The catching-up process suggests low economic growth rate in the high automatic technological product development to the Asian developing countries in the future.

Hence, the future economists predict that it views as probable successors of the Western world economic leadership if any Western country , such as UK manufacturers who prefer to invest to any high automatic technological products development , e.g. developing on human intelligence automatic technological products more than traditional common technological products development. On the one side, but it seems important to stress that two very poor countries among the challengers-China and India-are examples of countries that changed their institutions and economic policies from no or little economic freedom to more economic freedom. Because there two countries whose governments prefer to lend loans to encourage their country manufacturers prefer to invest high automatic technological products manufacturing. On the other side, attitudes toward foreign direct investment (FDI) have undergone change since the 1960 s and a large majority of less developed countries, e.g. China and India are now competing strongly among themselves and with developed market economies for direct investment from multinational companies. So, UK will face China and India high automatic technological product competitors in the future. And in fact, all countries that joined Western developed economies did that without much (if any) external inflow of public resources. It is right time that UK government needs to lend loans to encourage domestic manufacturers to invest high automatic technological products to raise whose international high technological products sale effort to win its future competitors. So, machine resources will be increased demand to o UK manufacturers if who chose to spend machine resources to innovate to manufacture any new and high technological automatic products to raise human daily life needs in the future. It means that it is right time UK manufacturers need buy much machines to prepare to manufacture many future high technological automatic products when these machine prices are low. Because the future global machine prices will possible be raised if many China and India manufacturers will also buy many machines in the future. For example, USA government had provided much financial support to assist sugar cane producers to develop their businesses. And they are dependent to a much larger extent than sugar cane producers and sugar processors in the USA on government. Without very high subsidies to renewable energy generation, they would not have survived at all. So, USA government had been the first country which could lent much financial assistance to encourage domestic renewable energy generation manufacturers to develop high technological energy manufacturing business. So, UK government needs follow USA to lend financial assistance to encourage domestic high technological automatic industry development.

Future economists also predict China and India will be competitors for future leadership in the global economy, special high technological products. China has been the media and analyst's favorite for quite some time. Quantitative projections have seemingly supported such expectation. Such as China and India had manufactured many high technological new space rockets products, ocean war large ships etc. Moreover, China has become one of the major world trade players in the early twenty-first century.

Many long-term forecasts, assuming similarly high economic growth rates in the decades ahead, predict that China will surpass the USA in terms of aggregate GDP somewhere between 2020 and 2030 or later, say between 2030 and 2050 year. The future economists conclude on the basis of these predictions that China will not only pass the USA in aggregate product (GDP), but its economy and economic policies will influence the rest of the world to a similar extent that the USA does at present.

I stressed a very important point, namely that the UK future high technological automatic product competitor China and India, namely that economies not only grow, but in the process change their structure. China and India have been industry very rapidly (the first transition) and building the physical infrastructure that accompanies industrialization changes to technology in the future. However, at a certain per capita GNP level the two countries, such as China and India will face another structural shift when which technological development will reach the mature stage in the future. China and India had been primarily historical pattern of economic development because the shift in the role of engine of growth from industry to services is to a much greater extent a qualitative shift. Both higher and different skills are required. And, even more importantly, interactions generating ideas driving the highly human-capital-intensive service economy require a much freer environment, not only in the economic area. Chinese exports have been heavily labor-intensive. This being the case, they contributed to the expansion of industrial employment, offering for the first time in the history of China a taste of (very modest) prosperity to more than 100 million new industrial workers and their families. This is the major component of the success accomplished by Chinese economic growth. Richer trade partners create room for more trade, so the Chinese should hope that intra-South trade, that is, trade between the emerging economies of Asia, the Middle East, Africa and Latin America, will open up new and growing opportunities. I presume that if Western economy , such as UK did not developed high technological automatic industry to stable their social welfare, so thoroughly slowed down their economic growth.

Will it allow China to accomplish the transition to a mature, innovation, service-sector-based market economy? It has allowed the economy to industrialize much more successfully, even if the labor shift from agriculture to industry has not yet been completed. But it is a long way off the next major test: the second high technological industry transition of the economic structure to China. Bear in mind that Russia attempted it twice and failed at both attempts.

But even, assuming that China at some point in the future does succeed in accomplishing the second transition, will it be able to supersede the USA, for example, as the main global high automatic technological innovation center if it wants to become the No.1 global high technological industry economy? Given the nature of the centralized state and its stability to collect financial resources , China's ability to increase research and development expenditure to high automatic technological products and to hire a mass of researchers, engineers, technicians and other specialists should not be doubted. This process in already taking place.

But , again, Soviet Russia already exceed the USA in the R&D/ GDP ratio in the 1970s, long before the communist collapse, with no effects on its innovativeness. Inputs matter less than outputs, quantity in the innovation process mean much less than quality.

The latter characteristics depends importantly on economic, civic and even political institutions. Otherwise, independent India had three options open to it in 1946s. It could pursue spontaneous economic development, with some state intervention to be sure, along the lines of basically free market capitalism; it could turn the clock back and try to recreate the rural-agricultural and handicraft based. The dominant way of thinking was Society -style priority to industrialization and , within industralization , priority to heavy industry. In other words, not textiles and clothing, which has been developing well in India since the mid- nine teen century, but production of sewing machines and , even better, production of machines the produce sewing machines.

The results were only to be expected. The heavy stress on the expansion of capital-intensive heavy industries in a very poor country quickly strained the ability of the Indian economy to generate adequate savings. Moreover, some of these industries were above the level of industrial competence of an underdeveloped economy. Thus, the amount of required resources (capital, skilled labor) was usually larger per unit of output than in the same industries in more mature, richer industries economies. In another view point, India will develop light industries, just as any other poor country with a great deal of unskilled labor, had a comparative advantage and no less importantly, an economy in which, due to their low capital/labor ratio, light industries could employ many more people, spreading prosperity more widely in a poor country. So, it explain that why China will have more effort to develop heavy high technological industry in the future. Thus, India got less economic efficiency, less employment than in a spontaneously developing economy, less ability to compete internationally in light industries suitable for an underdeveloped economy and finally got heavy industry unable to compete even on the domestic market and, therefore requiring no less heavy a dose of protection. Overall India got an underperforming economy, in particular in its relations with the rest of the world.

To conclude by comparing the performance of the traditional

sectors of the Indian economy and the performance of its modern, human -capital-intensive subsector of manufacturing and skill intensive service sector. The latter both employ workers with high- and medium -high skillful level (in branches ranging from computer software and biotechnology and pharmaceutical high technological light industry). India is ahead of China in terms of the output and export of such products and services. Thus, it implies that UK ought concentrate on developing high automatic heavy high technological industry, e.g. human intelligence technological products because these industry is not better development to other many countries' strong effort , such China and India large population countries.

Consequently, future (AI) robotic technology can be applied to medical service industry, e.g. in hospital and clinic environment to let patients to live in these places to feel more comfortable. It can also be applied to manufacturing industry to assist productivity performance rasing and computer software and biotechnology and pharmaceutical high technological light industry to improve computer technological software development and invention of much new biotechnology and pharmaceutical medicines for human health.

4 Increase development in genetics, human intelligence, robotics, nanotechnology, 3D printing and biotechnology technological industry

In US future, (AI) robotic tools will assist nanotechnology, 3D printing and biotechnology technological industry development, these kinds of jobs will be needed to increase development in genetics, human intelligence, robotics, nanotechnology, 3D printing and biotechnology. For example, smart systems homes, factories, farms grids or cities will help tackle problems ranging from supply chain management to climate change. The rise of US economy growth will allow US people to monetize everything from their empty house to their car in US. These new technological products development will change US patterns of consumption, production and employment adaption are also be changed by US corporations,

US government and individuals.

Why will the technological revolution be broader socio-economic, geopolitical and demographic drivers of change to influence future US social economic and consumption pattern change? Future US most occupations will also be changed. When some traditional old jobs are threatened by redundancy and other new technological jobs will grow rapidly, existing jobs are also changed in the skill sets required to do them. The debate is between some economists foresee limitless new job opportunities and foresee massive dislocation of US jobs. In fact, the reality is highly specific to future US high technological production industry, region and high technological occupation in question as well as how US production workers can be raised themselves ability to actions the upgrade level of high technological production ability from various stakeholders to manage high technological production method change.

Overall, this is a modestly positive outlook of US high technological production employment across future most high technological production industries with jobs growth expected in several sectors. However, it is also clear that this need for more talent in certain job categories is accompanied by high skills instability across all job categories. Combined together, future US net job growth and skills instability result in most US businesses with face major recruitment challenges and talent shortages, a pattern already evident in the result and set to get worse over next five years in possible.

The question is how US businesses, government and individuals will react to these new technological job changes, due to talent shortage, mass unemployment and growing inequality challenges will encounter in future US society.

The current technological revolution does not need become a race between humans and machines , but rather an opportunity for work to truly become a channel through which US people recognize their potential. So, if US traditional low manufacturing skillful workers lack talent to learn new skills to prepare to do future new technological manufacturing jobs, such as 3 D printing, robotics, nanotechnology, biotechnological high technological products manufacturing jobs. Then, it will cause increasing of unemployment rate to some not talent US low manufacturing skillful workers. So, US government or high technological product industry employers need to consider this future unemployment challenge will be caused by high technological products manufacturing changing influences. It seems high technological development will cause these low manufacturing skillful workers unemployed rising numbers as well as high manufacturing skillful workers human capital shortage global challenges will exist.

In the future, the driver of changes to influence US demographic and socio-economic growth. They may include: changing work environments and flexible working arrangements. It means new technologies are enabling workplace innovations , such as remote working, co-working spaces and teleconferencing. Rising of the middle class in Asia markets. It means the world's economic center is shifting towards the Asia developing countries.

Some economists predict that Asia will be projected to account for 66% of the global middle class and for 59% of middle class consumption by 2030 year. In addition, climate change, natural resource will be constraints to a greener economy. It means that climate change is a major driver of innovation as organizations search for measures to help adjust to its effects. As global economic growth consumers are needed to lead to demand for natural resources and raw materials, over explanation implies higher extraction most and degradation ecosystem and these challenges will also impact US employment changes needs. All US government also needs to concern future global economic change influence. Hence , future (AI) robotic tools will assist these industries' technological development and creates more new jobs.

Artificial Intelligent

Social Military Defense Weapon

Although (AI) can influence technological development to bring positive impact to bring beneficial welfare to provide human life. But, I also feel (AI) can bring new military to attack weak effort countries enemy from strong owning (AI) military defense wepon countries. If one day, some owning strong (AI) technological development countries' leaders who applied (AI) technology to manufacture social military defense weapon robots. Then, it will cause the third World war in possible. So, different countries' leaders need to consider (AI) invention ethic issue to keep world peace.

Nowadays, artificial intelligence (AI) is widely knowledge to be one kind of the dramatic technology. However, it is expected to continue, to have a disruptive impact on human's private and public life, so defense and security will be no exception. But how exactly will these be affected ? How will (AI) defense and security is incremental in nature?

To research why artificial intelligence (AI) has possible to be used to cause autonomous weapons by human. We need to understand these three aspects of relationship. They include cybersecurity and artificial intelligence and machine learning and autonomous weapon systems relationship between of them.

Firstly, we need to know what is the mean of artificial intelligence and cyber defense/offense? It means defense of critical networks: real time, pattern finding, anomaly seeking, it must utilize machine (AI) learning algorithms to efficiently, and instantaneously respond to potential network threats as well as it means human on or out of the loop. On the loop : it means anomaly detection: human notified, IT analysis, response. Out of the loop: it means anomaly detection: (AI) decides best method of response: quarantine, honey pot monitoring, hack-back. Thus, it is possible that (AI) can be used , such as autonomous cyber weapon.

What is artificial intelligence and autonomous weapons? Autonomous weapons mean one kind of weapon that can be selected and engaged a target, without intervention by a human operator. Are these machines artificially intelligent? I believe the answer is not, because present weapons systems are not capable of human level reasoning. But, (AI) algorithms are presently employed to process sensor data, monitor system health, take and respond to vocal commands manage data, navigate. This, future autonomous weapons systems will require stronger (AI) to be secure and operationally and cost effective. Moreover, self-aware autonomous cyber systems are crucial.

What is cybersecurity mean? It means the ability to control access to networked systems and the information they contain. It is acted to prevent , detect, recover, react. It is application objects concern people, process, technology and it's application goals are confidentiality, integrity and popular availability. Thus, what is cyber weapon mean? Walware means viruses, Trojans, zero-days, worms ransomware, spyware etc. Does it require a particular objective? E.g. military paramilitary or intelligence. Does it require physical harm? E.g. functional harm or interruption? Mental harm? Is (AI) a technological weapon that it is an object or tool? What about when it is an weapon agent?

In simplicity, (AI) can be one of scientific weapons platform. When one day, it is invented to be applied to control war planes to fly to any countries to attack enemies or it is invented to be seemed to human to replace soldiers to bring guns or any weapons go to other countries to attack. So, it is possible that future any war defense planes, (AI) technological automatic control weapon can be replaced of human soldiers or war plane pilots to control any war defense planes to go to different enemy countries to attack them easily. It is very horror matter to threaten global human's ourselves life in the future , if (AI) automatic control war defense planes or (AI) automatic control machine soldiers were invented successfully.

Hence , when (AI) can be applied to weapons platforms, it structures that launch weapons, i.e. jets, ships, vehicles. (AI) platform and weapon and software architecture components are be done one (AI) technological weapons systems. Thus, human will encounter any (AI) benefits or risks (threats) causes in the same time as soon as possible. If we can predict when (AI) weapon system will be manufactured or invented successfully. Then, we can reduce (AI) weapon systems risks , if we can threaten any (AI) scientists continue to invent any undiscovered (AI) weapons in any time to avoid the future first time (AI) weapon war occurrence in possible.

The (AI) weapon system risk means autonomy: the ability to problem solve technological war , when (AI) weapon system is manufactured successfully, the power to act, how to damage the (AI) weapon system. The power to chance to stop (AI) weapon system manufacturing processes, ability to create a new goals, how to change the (AI) weapon system inventors' or scientists' minds to avoid to apply (AI) tools to achieve attack goals to change to another positive goal. Due to human can't know a prior what an autonomous (AI) weapon system will do.

Although, human is known what (AI) is , but human is also known when (AI) scientists whose emergent behaviors will do to change to do any negative behaviors from positive behaviors. Whatever (AI) weapon system design we use, there will be cybersecurity, problems arising from computation design/ complexity. Due to any one (AI) scientist can manipulate the system to act against itself, or who can utilize traditional " cyber weapons" against the (AI) weapon system, or who can manipulate the system to lie to humans, but also due to complexity, there is no way to know if it is lying or not or bounded rationality : satisficing.

Finally, the most serious (AI) technological invention risks are human is unknown these aspects of (AI) absolutely: They are not simple automatic systems, learning reasoning, communication of " self-aware" systems. Thus, human will face (AI) technological invention risks or threats. We need to find any methods to avoid (AI) weapon system is manufactured successfully to avoid (AI) technological war can occur in future anyone day.

1 (AI) system immoral intention
Why (AI) system can be invented to damage our society ? IS it possible to achieve this (AI) damage system successfully? ON (AI)

attribution hand, it can be applied to cars, aircraft, which are subject to regulation designed to protect the public from harm and ensure fairness in economic competition. Thus, (AI) safety issue is important to scientists to consider.

IN general, the approach to regulation of (AI)-enabled products protect public safety issue should be informed by assessment of the aspects of risk that the addition of (AI) way reduce any respects of risk that it may increase. Also, where regulatory responses to the addition of (AI) threaten to increase the cost of compliance, or slow the development or adoption of beneficial innovations, policymakers should consider how those responses could be adjusted to lower costs and barriers to innovation without adversely impacting safety or market fairness.

For example, regulatory challenges that (AI) enabled present are found in the cases of automated vehicles. (AI)s, such as self-driving cars and (AI)-equipped unmanned aircraft systems. IN the long run, self-driving cars will likely save many lives by reducing driver error and increasing personal mobility, it will offer many economic benefits. Thus, public safety must be protected as these technologies are tested and begin to mature. Creating safe spaces and test beds for experimentation , and working with industry and civil society to evolve performance based regulations that will enable more uses as evidence of safe operation accumulates. Thus, it implies that any scientists can also invent (AI) system to control weapon defense planes or (AI) automatic machine human to do any soldier's behaviors to attack to any countries easily, instead of none driver automatic control vehicle invention. Thus, (AI) system can be applied to harm to human or achieve to damage our society aim by ourselves in possible.

The rapid growth of (AI) has dramatically increased the need for people with relevant skills to support and advance the field. AN (AI) −enables would demand a data literate citizenry that is able to read, use, interpret and communicate about data and participate in policy debates about matters affected by (AI). Thus, if (AI) technology is applied to assist human's social development and raising life enjoyment or benefits. It will bring positive impact to influence human's future life. Otherwise, if (AI) technology is unsafe to be applied to threaten human's society. It will bring negative impact to influence human's future life. Thus, (AI) scientists need to consider how to apply (AI) technology.

As (AI) technologies move toward deployment, technical expects, policy analysts and ethicists have raised concerns about unintended, consequences of adoption. Use one (AI) to make consequential decisions about people, often replacing decisions made by human –driven bureaucratic processes, leads to concerns about how to ensure justice, fairness, and accountability, the same concerns of human's safety issue. Thus,)AI) expects have cautioned that there are challenges in trying to understand and predict the behaviors of advanced (AI) systems.

Use of (AI) to control physical-world equipment leads to concerns about safety, especially as systems are exposed to the full complexity of human environment. A major challenge in (AI) safety is building systems that can safety transition from the closed world of the laboratory into the outside open world, when unpredictable things can happen. Adapting to unforeseen situations are difficult necessary for safe operation. Experience in building other types of safety artificial systems and, such as aircraft, power plants, bridges and vehicles has much to teach (AI) practitioners about verification and validation, how to build a safety case for a technology, how to manage risks, and how to communicate with stakeholders about risk. The risk means the harm of human's safety of (AI) damage system control machine invention. Thus, any (AI) scientists need consider moral responsibility when who decide to invent what kind of (AI) system machine to aim to bring human's benefits or attribute to human's welfare intention.

Thus, (AI) products safe invention matter will need any scientists' considerations. Because , if (AI) any products are unsafe or harm human's invention in the manufacturing process, it will bring any human's life danger when the (AI) system damage tools are invented successfully and are provided weapons to humans to use to attack other countries easily. It will cause future global human (AI) technological war occurrence.

I shall recommend the solution is necessary of ethical training for (AI) practitioners and students. Ideally, every student learning (AI) , computer science, or data science would be exposed to curriculum and discussion on related ethics and security topics. However, ethics alone is not sufficient. Ethics can help practitioners understand their responsibilities to all stakeholders, but ethical training should be methods for deciding good intentions into practice by doing the technical work needed to prevent unacceptable or immoral (AI) invention outcomes.

Hence, global human needs to concern (AI) weapon system invention security issue. Nowadays, (AI) has important application is increasing role for both defensive and offensive cyber measures. Currently, designing and operating secure systems requires significant time and attention from experts.

Challenges issues are raised by the potential use of (AI) in weapon systems. The United States has incorporated autonomy in certain weapon systems for decades, allowing for greater precision in the use of weapons and safer, more humane military operations. Nonetheless, direct human control of weapon systems involves some risks and can raise legal and ethical questions concern (AI) manufacturing process intention.

The key to incorporating autonomous and semi-autonomous weapon system into American defense planning is to ensure that U.S. Government entities are always acting in accordance with international humanitarian law, taking appropriate steps to control , to develop standards related to the development and use of such weapon systems. The United States has activity participated in ongoing international discussion on Lethal autonomous weapon systems and anticipates continued robust international discussion of those potential weapons systems. Thus, (AI) scientists have responsibilities to manage the potential to be a major driver of economic growth and social progress only, their (AI) intentions are not the global dominance aims absolutely, if (AI) product industry , civil society, government and the public work together to support (AI) positive development of the technology with thoughtful attention to its potential and to managing its invention threat risks to avoid (AI) products to manufacture to be used weapon tools.

Finally, I recommend that as the technology of (AI) continues to develop, practitioners must ensure that (AI) enables systems are governable, that what their inventions need to be openness to let public to know clearly and understandable; that they can work effectively with people and that their operation will remain consistent with human values and aspirations. Researchers and practitioners have increased their attention to these challenges , and should continue to focus on their future any (AI) inventions.

Hence, (AI) safe system ought to be applied to solve the biggest challenges that society faces, such as mobility for the elderly and those with disabilities, smart buildings may save energy and reduce carbon emissions, precision medicine may extend life and increase quality of life, smarter government may solve citizens more quickly and precisely., better protect those at any immoral invention risk and save money.

Moreover, (AI) enhanced education may help teachers give every child on education that opens doors to a secure and fulfilling life. Thus, these are the future human's potential benefits if the (AI) technology is developed to its benefits and scientists ought avoid to manufacture (AI) tools to cause weapon risks and challenges.

Consequently, the main point is that how experts invent (AI) systems. (AI) systems ought not be advanced weapon systems, it doesn't seem to be thought similar human soldiers mind and behaviors. (AI) system ought be systems that think like humans. (e.g. cognitive architectures and neural networks), systems that act like humans (e.g. pass the test via natural language process, knowledge representation, automated reasoning, and learning), systems that think rationally , e.g. logic solvers, inference and optimization and systems that act rationally e.g. intelligence software agents and embodies robots that achieve goals via perception, planning reasoning, learning , communicating, decision-making and acting function.

In conclusion, it is horror (AI) scientists will invent (AI) systems to be owned human's (soldier's) mind and attack strategic behavior to attack other countries easily, who must need to consider (AI) system ought be invented to own scientists' creating mind and non manual assistance functions for positive attribution to human's society. I expect that (AI) system can only be invented to create human's welfare in our future.

2 (AI) soldier weapon ethical, social and
economic negative impact

In the future, how human can avoid (AI) technological ethical, social and economic negative impact. Scientists need to concern these questions: how to develop of a good (AI) society, how the role and responsibility of the government, the private sector, and the reserch community(including education), in pursuing such a development, whether how the recommendation to support , such a (AI) system development may be in need of improvement.

However, none appers to deliver a comprehensive explicit vision of the role that (AI) system should play in mature information societies. Thus, (AI) 's potential contribution to social good shoud include an in-depth plan for linking in a comprehensive socio-political design questions of responsibility of the different stakeholders, of cooperation between them and of sharable values to understand of a good (AI) positive impact society, not a bad (AI) negative impact society.

Thus, the notion of mature information societies is introduced to stree the importance of addressing the current ethical challenges that (AI) poses in a comprehensive fashion.

It seems (AI) wil invention will be human's moral societal consideration issue. It concerns our (AI) scientists' moral issue, how who invent (AI) system to apply to which kind aspects. IF (AI) system was one direction on war weapon tools to similar to soldier's personal mind or attacking behavior. Then, it will bring poor social safety and poor economy growth our world, due to (AI) scientists' moral is low level.

Thus, the developed country US (AI) technological leader needs to focuse on the impacts of (AI)-driven customatin on the US job market and economy. It represents three specific policy responses to the perceived impact of (AI) on the US economy. They include these three aspects such as: How to invest in and develop (AI) for its many benefits, how to educate and train Americans for the jobs of the future and how to aid workers in the transition and empower workers to ensure broadly shared growth.

The future of (AI) influenced cyber conflicts need more than just the application of current and past solutions in order to ensure security and stability of societies, and avoid risks of escalation. To achieve this end, efforts to regulate cyber conflicts require an in-depth understanding of this new phenomenon, identify the changes brought about by cyber conflicts and the information revoluation, and defines a set of shared values that will guide the stakeholders operating to avoid the international (AI) war occurrence. This becomes clear when considering for example, cyber deterrence. Deploying conventional (cold war) strategies to deter (AI)-influenced cyber conflicts proves highly problematic and the urgent need to foster and coordinate new solutions able to account for the any kinds of conflicts of the cyber demain and of mature information societies to avoid (AI) technological war occurrence in the future.

We hope that in the on-going international conversations and reviews, the US government with further specify how " (AI) system invention law" fit into their vision of the future of society in this case the future of (AI) technological war and conflicts. Hence, (AI) scientists need to concern ethical issues related to (AI), like fairness, accountability and social justice can be addressed through increasing needs. Such as: how the creation of a new body focused on robotics and related (AI) system development to avoid to intent to apply weapon tools to provide advice on the policy, legl and consumer protection issues arising in these fields should be considered.

How to achieve ethical training of (AI) staff and ethical education of the public is certainly important responsibility for (AI) tools ethical behavior and design to the private sector and the citizens : of unique challenges that (AI) brings to society in terms in fairness, social equity and accountability are addresses. Thus, the development of the (AI) technology and defining good (AI) remains problematic. In particular, the US government's innovation driven approach to defining the potential, positive impact of (AI) shows that more could be done to ensure that the opportunities and advantages brought about by (AI) are shared by all society.

An initial on Robotics, based upon the ethical framework and guiding principles is proposed. It should be complementary to legislaton and comprise ethical codes of conduct for Robotics researchers and designers, codes for research ethics committees as well as licenses (rights and duties) for designers and users. Thus, (AI) robotics invention of safety issues is very important considertion to any (AI) inventions or researchers. Every country's government ought have legal guiding to control their robotics' manufacturing intention. If their robotics (AI) is applied to seem to be soldiers to attack other countries to threaten their people's safety. Then, those (AI) inventors or researchers need to be punished by law.

In conclusion, I believe (AI) technology will be applied to weapon, when it's technological development is nearly mature to able to learn human's mind to do any behavior. During (AI) technology reachs thie mature stage, I predict the (AI) weapon tool , e.g. (AI) soldiers will have chance to be caused. This (AI) invention mature stage has these characteristics such as:

When (AI) invetion reachs this mature stage, computers and robots will develop conscious, intelligent, personified minds. Further, information technology devices and (AI) systems will be implanted into humans, enhancing, psychological and behavioral abilities and allowing for direct communication with artificial intelligent minds. There will be both artificial intelligence (AI) and intelligence amplification (AI) in the relatively near future stage.

During the (AI) invention reachs this mature stage, these will be an ongoing mulit-faceted integration of information technologies and human life. Humans and information technology will cooperate. Humans will increasingly immerse their lives and minds in (AI) systems of technological intelligence and virtual reality. The distinction between humanity and technology will increasingly close dependence.

During the (AI) invention mature stage reachs that the environment will be infused with information technology, becoming animated, communicative and more intelligent. The destinction between the artificial and the natural will increasing close dependence.

During the (AI) invention mature stage will expand through virtual reality, simulated and virtual reality will increasingly into normal reality, e.g. the (AI) weapons is virtual reality to seem to be soldier weapon.

Finally, during the (AI) invention mature stage is as the global expression of the evolving human-technology integration a " world brain" and " world mind" will emerge on the earth. This psychophysical (AI) weapon system will enhance and enrich the capacities of both individual and collective cogniton. This (AI) weapon system is a potential starting point toward the evolution of a cosmic brain and cosmic mind.

Thus, it is possible that the workship raw data was a unique way in which (AI) could be weaponized to cause war, during the (AI) invention stage reachs the invention mature stage. However, (AI) weapon manufacturing factory will be built possibly. In the future, how will we defins and locate (AI) weapon factories. Especially, as these factories are no longer solely buildings , but a mil of virtual and substantially different facilities, particularly as it shifts from a physical assemly and development model to a distributed and flexible network. Needing minimal raw materials to develop (AI) weapons, the phsysical location of their (AI) factories could be anywhere and their identification from the outside, nearly impossible. Given the expanding uses for intelligent and super-intelligent (AI). How will we tell the different form a location that is manufacturing (AI) for the creation of weapons versus creating (AI) for an innovative new gaming platform?

In conclusion, human needs to consider every (AI) scientist's personal ethical or moral mind and research intention and (AI) system invention of (AI) weapon factories cause. During (AI) invention reachs the mature stage if human expects to avoid (AI) technological war occurrence in future one day. The technological development on autonomous military robots, ideally among relevant social groups and actors including human-rights, activists, researchers developers, engineers, philosophers, policy-makers, military authorities, lawyers, journalists and the publis need to consider when human has effort to invent autonomous military robots successfully in the future one day. Finally, some ambitious countries or dominant global countries must like to apply (AI) autonomous military robots to be machine soldiers more than human soldiers if (AI) technology had reached the mature stage. So, future (AI) autonomous military robots will be the next choice of weapon to follow nuclear weapon. If civilians were used as a human (AI) soldiers, the weapon simply ignored them and targeted anyway. This scenario highlighted the dangers of proliferation and quick replication of autonomous weapons. Unlike nuclear weapon, a piece of code for (AI) artificial intelligent soldier could be obtained on the black market and replicated at little cost and the hardware for this type of weapon doesn't require costly or hard to obtain components and materials. Thus, (AI) artificial intelligent soldiers can be manufactured many at cheaper cost. Otherwise, manufacturing one nuclear bomb weapon will spend too much cost. Hence , it is possible that (AI) artificial intelligent soldier will be future new technological weapon to follow nuclear bomb weapon. Hence, any country government needs to legislate to control any (AI) scientists' inventions whether they are attributed benefits or welfares to human or damage human's safety.

(AI) assist future computer

industry new gender innovation development

Why China's computer manufacturing and product development industry will be global leader to compete US computer dominant market. The reason is because that China will have possible to dominate global computer industry development if it can invent new (AI) learning tool to assist global computer systems to raise more efficient performance effort.

Nowadays, China's computer industry is the largetest hardware producer production and experts is dominated by Taiwanese firms. It is also the second largest personal computer (pc) market and domestic pc companies are top three sellers in global computer manufacturing and product development market. Forx example, Lenovo buys BM pc business in 2004 year. It implies US, IBM pc manufacturing leader can not dominate global computer market in possible in the future.

Reed Electronic Research, Yearbook Of World Electronic Data (2003) indicated that the leading computer producing countries of hardware production in US \$millions and share share of total gogal production: The world region US was the global rank number one. In 1995 year, US had US \$76,284 value, market value 26.5%. Then in 2000 year, US had increased up to US \$ 90, 430 value, market share 24%. Till to 2003 year, US had fallen down to US \$ 69,102 value, market share 21.7%. However, US hardware production was still the global rank number one , although its hardware production value had been falling down. But, the following second rank country, Japan and the third rank country, Singapore and the fourth rank country, Taiwan and the fifth rank county China which hardware production value could not exceed US till to 2003 year. However, although China had the lowest hardware production value US \$5,600 to compare to among of these countries in 1995 year, but China had increased the value to US \$65,000 and market share to 20.5%. Otherwise, Japan, Singapore and Taiwan value and market share had surprisingly fallen down below than China value in 2003 year. Thus, it seemed that China will be a potential country to compete US hardware production industry after 2003 year.

Reed Electronic Research, Year book Of World Electronic Data (2003) also showed that these computer companies of China had these % of market share : Beijing Founder had 9.9%, Tsinghua Tongtang had 7.8%, dell had 7.2 % , IBM had 5.1% , HP had 4.8% of market share. Thus, it also seemed that China some computer companies will have impotant large market share percentage in global pc sale market. In the future, global hardware production and pc sale industry. China and Taiwan both countries will be one pc manufacturing and design and sale partner. The reason is that China and Taiwan had been the number one rank of markers of notebook pcs, motherboards, scanners, keyboards, add-on card optical drives, monitors and some network equipment etc. pc (personal computer) relative computer function products. It seems that these both countries had co-operated to research any computer relative products to sell to global computer market. They are also the original design manufacturers (DDMS) develop and manufacture over half the world's notebook pcs as well as their customers include all major branded pc vendors (OEMS).

Taiwan Minstry Of Economic Affairs (2003) indicated Taiwan's top notebook ODMS include: In 2003 year volume (thousands) Quanta had $8,500 sale volume thousands , for example, Quanta major OEM partners include Gateway, Dell, HP, IBM, Apple , Sharp, Sony, Fujitsu-Siemens (F/S). Compal had $6,000 sale volume (thousands) , Compal major OEM partners include Dell, HP, F/S, Toshiba, Acer. Thus, it also implied Taiwan had many small size and non famous brand of computer companies which choose to co-operate to be partners with some global large size and famous brand of computer companies to raise competitive effort in global computer market, such as Dell, IBM, HP, Gatway, Apple etc.

Thus, the future trend of computer new product manufacturing development will shift from US to Taiwan and SE Asia, then to China. However, what kind of knowledge work factors will be needed to China and Taiwan . In general, notebook manufacturing stages will include: The first process is design stage, it includes concept design, such as analyze need, create concept and set brand image as well as product planning, such as business case, specifications, industrial design and sourcing strategy. The second process is development stage, it includes design review steps, such as design review, such as mock-ups, electrical test as well as prototype build, such as commercial samples, integrated system test as well as pilot production, such as production process design, pilot. Final process is production stage, it includes mass production, such as ramp-up, volume production, production testing and global distribution as well as sustaining support, such as speed bump, component replacement, technical support and warranty support. Thus, I believe that China and Taiwan must own thee knowledge work skillful of computer design and development professionals who can assist these two countries how to innovate their future computer development to change global traditional computer model to be renew and innovate computer model in the future.

Due to computer industry's stages of development and manufacturing are closely linked , need manufacturability , testing of sample products, concept design and product planning stay together in lead markets and branded vendors, design and development can be separated organizationally and geographically. Thus, China and Taiwan choose to co-operate to exchange their different skill, such as either China has own more concept design and product planning skill or more development skill or more production skill. Then, China will choose either one of the most beneficial comparative advantage among of them. To bring this one of the most beneficial co-operative advantage to attract Taiwan to choose either one of the beneficial comparative advantage of skill, such as either design or development or producton to already co-operate to compete the Western developed country US together.

Thus, US won't be the global computer industry development leader if both US country famous and large employee number computer companies, such as IBM and Apple which choose to outsource their pc design and development and production skill to

China and Taiwan both countries to help them to develop global computer design and development and production skill to be upgraded. Thus, I feel these both countries will plan how to co-operate to compete US to win the global computer industry leader position in the future.

When China invented its (AI) learning system success. Why does it influence global computer industry market change? For example, in the future, instead of global computer manufacters need to consider the design, development and production processes, who also need to consider what factors can influence consumers' laptop purchases. Because any consumers have much different computer model and brand to choose to make final decision to buy any computers. If the computer manufacturer can predict what factors will be whose weakness(es) to influence global computer consumers to change whose mind or attitude to choose to buy other brands of computers, then it won't lose its many old computer customer numbers and reduces it market share in global computer market share.

Nowadays, in general computer has three kinds to provide to global consumers to choose to buy , such as laptop, notebook computers, desktops. it seems that laptop and notebook computers and desktops will have different factors to influence any consumers to choose to buy any brand of computer products. Thus, computer indsutry can divide three consumer groups, such as (stayers, satisfied switchers and dissatisfied switchers) of a computer company with respect to the factors influencing consumers' laptops or notebook computers or desktops purchases. However, I feel the factors can include such as core technicl features, post purchase services, prices and payment conditions, peripheral specification, physical appearance, value added features and connectivity and mobility seven main factors that are influencing consumers' laptop or notebook computer or desktop purchases in global computer industry market.

Ganesh et al., (2000) indicates the customer base of a company consists of three groups of consumers: stayers, satisfied switchers and dissatisfied switchers. Therefore, the consumers in this study replied to the question about whether the current brand that who were using was their first laptop brand or whether who had switched from a previous laptop brand. As a following question, consumers who had switched were asked to state the reason of why who switched from a previous laptop brand brand to their current brand. The options include overall dissatisfaction from the previous laptop brand and reasons other than dissatisfaction. Thus, computer companies need to know what factors influence either whose prior computer customers why who don't choose repeat to buy its any computer products or whose new potential computer customers why who don't choose to buy its any computer products in the first time choice. Thus, future computer manufacturers need to consider intangible salespeople service attitude or performance, such as salespeople current purchase and post purchase service, e.g. technical repair, model function explanation how to use the computer, instead of tangible product performance, e.g. computer appearance design , function , mobility and internet and document download speed connectivity function. Because salespeople and technicians' service performance can be represented to the computer image. If they can provide excellent service to let computer buyers to feel satisfactory, then they can help their computer company employer to build good image. So, staff service performance will be one important factor to influence computer consumers to make the final decision to choose to buy the brand of computer products more easily. Even, one famous brand computer company, such as IBM, Apple, Gateway, these any one of famous brand computer company must not attract any new (the first time) or repeat computer buyers to choose to buy their any kind of computer products , such as laptop, desktop or notebook more easily due to their famous brand. Althoug, these famous computer companies had built good image to let consumers have more confidence to buy any kind of their computer products. But, if these famous computer companies' salepeople or repair technicians can not provide excellent customer service or performance to satisfy their computer buyers' service need, e.g. explaining how to use the new computer, repair post purchase service etc. I believe these famous brands of computer consumers will not have more desire to prefer to chose to buy any one of these famous computer brand's products. Otherwise, if the other less famous computer companies' any kind of laptop, desktop or notebook sale price is higher than the famous brand of computer companies' products sale price, but their salepeople or technicians can provide more excellent service attitude or performance to satisfy their consumers' needs. It is possible that the new or first time computer buyers or repeat computer buyers will still choose to buy their computers. So, the famous or less famous computer brand is not one important factor to influence the computer buyer to decide either to buy the computer or not buy the computer. Otherwise, computer company's salepeople and repair technician whose service performance or attitude will be one important intangible factors to influence any first time (new) or repeat computer consumers to choose to buy any famous or less famous brand of computer company's product, instead of the tangible computer design appearance and reliable function and convenient mobility and long term durability etc. factors influences.

Thus, China has possible to influence global office and home computer comsumers to choose to buy its any brands of computers to use if it can invent (AI) learning systems to assist global computers to raise their performance efficiency. So, it will influence global computer consumers to choose its country's any brands of computers to buy to use, due to themselves new (AI) learning computers can help office and home computer users to raise efficiency and provide the excellent productive performance to them more than the traditional computers.

1 Can culture factor influence the (AI)
computer consumer choice?

When China's (AI) computer learning system has developed in success. Then, it will possible to influence global consumers' traditional computer applying culture to change to new innovation

(AI) learning computer applying culture. It means that China will dominate global computer consumer choice to be trended to choose to buy China's any computer brands' produducts , due to it 's (AI) technology can be invented to apply to traditional computers in order to raise their efficiency and reduce office staffs' workload and provide excellent performance to serve office or home (AI) learning computer users.

Durmza and Zengin, (2011:53) indicted marketers closely interested in this issue to know the family which changed and renewed in course in time. It provides an advantage for a marketer to know the family structure and its consumption characteristics. Nowadays, consumer behavior is influenced not only by consumer personalities and motivation, but also by the relationships within families. Family is a social group and it can be considered a crucial place in th perception of marketing (Durmaz, Yakup, CELLK, Mucahit and ORUC, Reyhan, (2011).

The consumer buying behaviors examined through an empirical study. Then, it brings this question: Whether cultural factors will influnece the computer consumer choice. Choice and include computer brand choice, computer price choice, computer model choice, computer design choice, laptop or desktop or notebook product choice, new or second-hand old computer choice, the computer of manufacturing country choice, computer package choice etc. So, any consumer will consider to choose any one of these to decide to buy which kind of computer.

Every country computer consumers had different culture to influence their computer shopping choice. I feel culture can be explained how to influence to computer shopping such as: How do the country computer consumers buy and use their computer products habitually ? How do the country computer consumers react to th computer price changes, attractive advertising methods to satisfy whose needs and computer company sany store interiors? What underlying mechanisms operate to produce any one of the country computer consumers' responses? If computer marketers have answers to such these questions, who can make better managerial decisions how to adopt which computer target country (countries) consumers' culture.

Consumer behavior deals with many other issues, for instance (Priest, Carter and Statt, 2013: 19). How do we get information about products? How do we assess alternative products? How do different people choose or use different products? How do we decide on value for money ? How much risk do we take with what products? Who influences our buying decisions and our use of the product? How are brand loyalties formed and changed? For computer industry, it means that how computer consumers get information about computer products, how computer consumers assess alternative notebook, desktop, laptop computer products, how different age, country, culture, sex, student or working people or retired people computer consumers choose or use different kind of computer products, such as notebook, desktop, laptop computer products, how much risk computer consumers take with notebook, desktop, laptop computer products, the computer consumers' buying decisons and their use of the desktop or notebook or laptop computer products will be influenced by whom, e.g. family, friends, teacher, employer, computer salepeople, advertisement marketer etc. , computer company brands how are formed and changed by whom, e.g. computer consumers, computer company competitors, marketers, different countries' culture etc.

Durmaz and Jablonski, (2012:56) also explained culture is the essential character of a society that distinguishes it from other cultural groups. The underlying elements of every culture are the values, language, myths, customs, laws and the artifacts or products that are transmitted from one generation to the next (Lamb, Hair and Deniel, 2011: 371). Culture is the most fundamental determinant of a person's wants and behavior. Whereas, lower creatives are governed by instinct, human behavior is largely learned. The child growing up in a society leans a basic set of values, perceptions, preferences and behaviors through a process of socialization involving the family and other social roles. So, I feel different country have different culture to influence as well as different country computer consumers who have different computer purchase and consume habitually. So, computer manufacturers ought focus on manufacturing the unique need and characteristics to satisfy any country's consumers' needs.

What is my idea about future global computer competition and factors influence computer consumer behavior ?

In conclusion, future computer industry development will trend that computer manufacturers need to consider every country's computer comsumer culture. Because every country computer consumers who will have different computer consumption habitually if who can predict what the country most computer consumers culture, then they can have more confidence to sell their computers to different country markets. Moreover, US computer manufacturers need to consider China and Taiwan computer manufacturing technology because it is possible that these both countries will be its main competitor among different computer manufacuring countries. Because thess both countries will cooperate to research new model of different computers to attract global computer consumers to choose to buy their new model of computer products in the future. Finally, computer manufacturers need to consider salepspeople and repair technicians service performance because computer consumers will consider intangible service performance , instead of tangible computer quality and price and style etc. factors . The main reason is that any computer have chance to be needed to repair and salespeople' skill will influence the computer consumer to make final decision to choose to buy the brand of computer. Thus, these factors will influence global computer development and trend in the future.

Artificial Intelligent Robot: Technology change traditional production of factor model

1 What is mean of (AI) Technological innovation production of factor ?

Can (AI) robot technological learning system change future traditional production of factors model: land, human, equipment and capital to any organizations in order to replace these production of factors and assist organizational development efficiently and effectively?System may be physical , like the solar system or an ecological system or which may be simply behavioral, like an organization. For example, a national economy may be a system, markets are systems, firms and factories are systems. Even, families and individuals are economic systems. The economy of the largest systems, national economy, may be called macroeconomy, which deals in terms of national aggregates for output, income, productivity. The economics of small systems, which are their parts or subsystems may be called microeconomics.

This is traditional production of factor model. for example, a system transforms inputs into outputs. An economic system is such a process. For example, factories are as systems take in raw materials, services etc. and change them into products for sale, i.e. output and consume them, thereby transforming them into rubbish, incidential is bad output. Also, countries consume their actural resources to enhance their standard of living and change them into waste products. If the system in question is national economy, some of the subsystems are might consider to be: the government, the firms, the consumers, the natural resources which it has at its disposal. Each subsystem is itself composed of subsystem of a lower order, such as a firm and each of these can be decomposed into further subsystems, depending on the purpose of the analysis. " All subsystems" interact need have individual characteistics, i.e. they are synergistic if they expected to raise producivity or efficiency or effectively. So, it needs high technological assistance to raise whose ability in economic view.

However, an economic system must continually adapt and restructure to meet the challenges of a changing economic environment if it is to prosper. For example, a firm must respond to its environment in the form of it customers' needs threats from its competitors, government regulations etc. Nowadays, technological innovation process and the nature of social economic and social changes which is occurring as the same time. So, organizations need to have strategic management to raise technological innovation to achieve raising productivity and efficiency aim. In the futue, (AI) robots will be possible one kind of new production of factor to assist organizational development and raise manufacturing efficiency and staffs' working performance in every team.

2 How does (AI) technological innovation occur in economic process?

What is economic process? It consists of the production and consumption of products and services by human. It is a process devised by human for own benefit pupose only. In the past, human lack advanced technological invention, e.g. family society required a much greater degree of organizational skill than hunting and gathering, it seems farming society does not need to achieve efficiency or productivity aim, because it is not industralized manufacturing society. Nowadays, the investment of resourcs is required for manufacturing processes for factories. The manufacturing stage thus needs machines, but it extends the economic process into the processing of manufacturing things, such as food. So, the knowledge and skills to do this are much more specialized again than farmer's or hunter's. So, technological innovation is needed to raise efficient productivity in factories, e.g. the increasing skills of manufacturing and the use of more intensive energy resources, such as coal and oil, gas, even solar energy either resources are from the sun or resources are from earth, e.g. fuels , heat, light, sound utilitiesm liquids , gases,solids. So, technological innovation is important to influence our economic development in our societies.

Economists usually classify what who call future of production into land, labor and capital. Why technological innovation is one another factor of production. For example, the economic process indicates that the first step is resources from the earth, e.g. solar energy supplies to earth to satisfy human needs. In the economic process, it needs these both supplies, driving force of transformation energy supply and captalyst , such as skills, knowledge, organization, creativity, creative participation in consumptions supply. Then, manufacturers shall change these both supplies to production and distribution of ordered materials and utilities in the economic process. Finally, it will provide to human consumption and human spent resources returned to earth in the final step. Another example of the elements of the economic process: the input is driving force of transformation stage of energy sources, e.g. sunlight firewood, oil and gas, coal , nuclear and household and industrial waste. Next is the economic process stage: facilitators, it includes tangible facilitator includes skills, knowledge, organization, creativity, e.g. language, science, technology, industry, machine, politics, law and order, defence, strategic plan, information systems, administration, tangible facilitator includes incentive system, e.g. money, banking, insurance, shares, private or public organizations, markets, land area. Finally, is the product of innovation stage, it includes utilities , such as electricity , heat, light, sound, motive power as well as ordered materials (products) , such as bread, meat, mine, shoes, clothes, houses, television, roads (public goods) etc. In future, (AI) robotic development will be possible participate to new economic process in order to raise global efficiency and performance for every businesses.

3 How (AI) robotic innovation information factor influences the product successful sale

What is the role of (AI) robotic innovation information (big data gathering method) ? Any markets requires product or service suppliers rationally act on the basic such information. But what who can't know in advance is how all the other participants are going to behave. The market clearing price would already be known. There would in fact be agreed prices and which everything could be exchanged, and there would be no market system at all. And so who come to market to settle the price/quantity relationship. The theory is that which will arrive at a single price and quantity which reflect supply and demand. However, the number of interactions or pieces of information to be transmitted doubles with every new participants. However, the requirement for information is not limited to the particular market in question. A compromise between the number of people needed to make more nearly " perfect" in the economic sense, and the quantity of information needed to allow it to arrive at a unique price/quantity relationship. The concept of degrees of freedom is widely used in different technological forms, e.g. engineering industry, the equipment is used by manufacturers to make pencils will be worn out to some extent in the process, and this forms an energy path straight to earth from the market in which the equipment was bought. Similarly wear and tear on the equipment used to make the intermediates and the raw materials will also form direct paths to earth from the markets in which were bought. It seems technological innovation factor of production can bring the pencil stationery product innovation when the new pencil stationey product is produced the more excellent quality by the new machines innovation.

In an economic system which is working " perfectly" according to the definitations, output is therefore a function of available energy and the technological skills to apply it to conversion of inputs into materials and utilities . In a market economy, given the availability of inputs of energy and materials, and the necessary information, the only factor which can bring this about in the long term is a change in the energy efficiency of its conversion process, i.e. the energy consumed unit of output of the same total production. This depends in the application of skills and design, that is technology factor of production.

Why (AI) big data gathering information can influence product sale ability. For example, the commodity is technologically complex like a computer, an aircraft or even a refrigetator. One is buying not just the piece of equipment, but also its specification because few people would understand the parts of the machine, let alone be able to judge their quality. Furthermore, one is also buying the future performance of the machine in operationm , its fuel consumptionm reliability, service costs, length of life, resistance to obsolescence etc. Probably the only guarantee that any information obtained on these points is valid is the reputation of the manufacturer. Purchasers estimate chose chances of surviving the guarante period. Brand names are a way of simplisfying information flows. Such problems of defining the commodity and so handling the information necessary to arrive at a stable price, are magnified when counterfeit products, such as are flooding on to the market at present, find their way into markets for genuine products. Buyers will be unable to distinguish unless who are experts and sometimes that may need chemical analysis or destructive testing. This is a recent phenomenon to buy technological products.

4 Why does (AI) big data gathering information technology influence the real market system change ?

Can (AI) big data gathering information technology be one kind of production of factor to influence the real market system change to be more fast speed of market information communication in global industries? The market system in the real world includes: the first is manual work (manpower) element, in effect the provision of an elementary utility for consumption in a conversion process. If labors are not providing manpower, who become unemployed. Unemployment is not simply leaving a resource at a particular time, it is an injustice and a burden one the very real society which economics is supposed to help. Moreover, the unemployed can't spend the money who don't earn, and so buyers are reward from the economic process. The second is catalytic skills, knowledge, organization and creativity element which applied to the conversion processes which turn raw materials into products and utilities for consumption. In this case, who are as varied as the individuals that make up mankind, their accumulated knowledge, their capability of organising themselves to achieve their ends and not least their creativity,the ability to generate entirely new catalytic effects. Finally, is the incentive element, which is the prospect of participating in comsumption of the products of the economic process. The incentive system is cash for current or future exchange for products and utilities. The incentive system must be within the control of the social system of which it is a part. It can only be addressed by society as the whole system. However, for the individual and the firm too the creative must by definition come from outside and it is also depend on the rest of society.

What kinds of product can link between markets to increase speed of market information communication when global industries choose to apply (AI) big data gathering information technology to gather global competitors' product and client and price etc. business data. However, there are products which are linked in a different way by associated use. For products anyone who buys a vehicle must also be prepared to buy its fuel, tyres etc. A decision to buy the vehicle therefore automatically generates subsequent expenditure in the other markets. These markets are not so much competitors for buyers' money as complementary to each other. Sale in one must lead to sales in the other. This technological products have the same point, it is that which are needed to attempt to innovate their quality to raise their competitive ability to win their competitors. It seems that (AI) big data gathering information technological innovation can be a factor production to these different brands of vehicles and which related link products. Much the same occurs in technological industry. A company may feel that it is wise to buy related pieces of equipment from the same manufacturer, especially if they have to be connected in some way, whatever the price, within reason.

5 Can (AI) big data gathering timing of information influence real marketing system?

The analysis has shown that two sorts of (AI)big data gathering information are essential of the market is to reach " equilibrium" values of price and quantity: information concerns on the economic environment, which participants can obtain before the market opens; and information about the process of bargaining displayed, which can only be made available as the bargaining proceeds. However, buyers and sellers happen next. If the information acts as a reference point, it can only be a historical one. This is particularly so where markets operate continuously. There is always a lapse between the conclusion of deals and their display, so that new deals are always influenced to be not update information , in the absence of the most recent data, if dealing is busy. So, timing of information ought to be kept the most update to let buyers can have more confidence to make final choice to buy the broad of products. The quality of information which had to passed during bargaining in order to achieve on a unique price/quantity relationship increased rapidly with the number of participants because of the need of to allow everyone of buyers to interact with all the others.

It follows therefore, that as the number of participants becomes very large, the necessary information flows become much larger still and the time needed to allow this to take place increases greatly. So, timing of information can influence the participants would have changed or would have not changed their minds or gone home before proceedings could draw to a close. So, price and quality is the main message of information to influence consume individual attitude to decide to buy the product in market.

Timing of information can influence business cycles. It is well known that business activity is cyclinal. The short cycles of 4 to 5 years are best established , but consumers believe who can discern longer term and even very long term cycles of activity with periods of up to 50 years. Cyclical behavior, can only occur where these is an imperfect response to change, because of imperfect information. In general, this sort could not caused by the response time behavior of individual markets. Whatever the nature of the link, it is clearly the case that the price/quality relationship in individual markets is varying independently of the factors which might normally be expected to affect it in isolated systems. So, cyclical phenomena in business are strong evidence of the market process network behaving as a system.

In conclusion, markets are activites to exchange products and services. The elements of economic chains together to allow modern industrial economies or (AI) big data gathering information technological economy to function with all their complexity. They are essential to change and they permit innovation. However, markets are not well represented by the conventional supply/demand schedules, in particular because these can not include the effects of time as an variable factor. It is much clear to represent timing of information as systems in the form of flow diagrams showing the movement of products from innovative processes through markets to consume. Revenue from the market then supplies feedback to product manufacturers, and the whole system responds at different rates to different levels of feedback from clients. An effective medium of exchange is necessary for proper responses to be made. The complexity of the modern world, where price and quantity and quality in the market are all can't exist without the timing of information factor influence. Price signals are often confused by products, imperfect or incomprehensible information and the various effects of time, and in any case quantities to be supplied to the market have to be decided well in advance of market day. The whole trend a modern industrial economy or technological economy is towards product differentiation. Such as mobile phone, laptop computer etc. technologic products. Manufacturers often need to innovate design, quality, functions to adapt to client's individual need. So, technological innovation is often a production of factors to invent high technological products. Services too can't be fitted into price/ quantity schedules because it is impossible to define the product. Otherwise, the categorisation of human as labor, having a price/ quantity relationship, when who are clearly , each is an individual learning system, changing every day of whose life and changing the economic process accordingly. In fact, human must necessarily be accepted as a feature of modern life, to protect to let them to enjoy high quality of life. So, individual economic stage will be needed to enter technological economic stage in economic environment. Indeed by limiting the rate of change such actions may in no small measure be a condition of stability for the people in an economy . It seems that (AI) big data gathering information technological innovation is one factor of production and it has close relstionship to timing of reasonable price and quality information to persuade consumers to choose to buy the manufacturer's product.

6 (AI) big data gathering information can reduce the cost basis of economic activity to any businesses

(AI) big data gathering information technology can help any organizations to reduce the time and human effort economic cost. In conversion processes there is always some wear and tear of the fixed asset, the equipment, building etc. which reduce their capacity to produce in future. Of course after the money has been spent on the plant, it is no longer cost of operating. This is not technological obsolescence which results from development of better ways of meeting market needs. The efficiency of produrers is continually improved and the most effective use of the resources available is continually improved and the most effective use of the resources available to the society, and the most effective use of the resources available to the society is made according to the criteria of economic values. The under-utilised resources locked up in the inefficient operation are not necessarily lost. The producer may learn in time to use them better. So that who can eventually compete on moral equal terms, or who may give way to another who knows how to manage the resources more efficiently. If however, the inefficiency has a deep-rooted cause which can not be remedied, or even a producer who is capable of improvement but refuses to act, then the resources run down to extiaction faster than ordinary wear and tear would cause them to. So, it suppose to technological innovation can help producers to reduce cost for long term. It is cost benefit to producers for long term.

For agricultural industry example, it was said that the only way for a farmer to increase whose not revenue significantly, once who was farming as efficiently as possible, was to increase the area of land under cultivation. But technological innovation is such production of factor, it might be a case for increasing the area under cultivation in order to make better use of a piece of equipment, such as a tractor, and so spread its cost over more production. Another might be in the processing industries, such as petrochemicals or oil where many new producers with the same global threats and opportunities. The input costs when products or utilities move in the direction of time and energy in the economic process. If one opportunity for using the resources is selected, then another potential use will be foregone. Opportunity costs are therefore distinguished from input costs by time. So, the production for factor of technological innovation can be opportunity cost, if the manufacturer felt who can spend less manufacturing expenditure for long term. Due to who lose to use money to spend other expenditure or invest, who choose to invent technological innovation to reduce long term input costs. The best opportunities are those which maximise prices and minimise costs. SO, (AI) big data gathering technology can be applied to argicultural industry to help farmers to reduce farming time and farming equipment cost to grow any fruit, vegetable and rise , tomotato , potato etc. food in production of factor view.

Producers try to achieve higher market prices by giving their products some distinguishing feature which whose hope will attract buyers away from other competitors and /or generate new buyers, what marketers call product differentiation. In effect they try to move their product into a new market, perhaps thought of as " up market" or a " market niche", but certainly in separate market for analytical purpose. Even if they can not do this, which is unusual in these days of increasing technological innovation and communication , operators continually try to improve their processes in order to reduce costs. If always requires the investment of new resources, e.g. technological innovation.

In the real world, it is not possible to differentiate products or processes except in time. The overall result is to move the process in the direction of economic improvements, in effect the behavior of economic system as a learning system. Time introduces all the risks and opportunities which present themselves to the processor. In the analysis which follows , we classify and illustrate the various aspects of economy of scope under the traditional economic heading of labor, capital, and land. Energy and information, technological innovation are considered too ,because which are fundamental to all systems and process in economic activity.

7 The (AI) big data gathering technological innovation benefits

First, (AI) big data gathering technological innovation can bring to help organizations to reduce staff number and divide labor to raise different department work efficiency and performance benefits. For the division of labor benefits example. This is a complex process into stages in which a worker can specialize, thus allowing who to perform that particular task more efficiently, i.e. at lower cost per unit of effective output than if who had to undertake the whole process. Such an improvement in efficiency results from the more effective learning, greater development of skills and more intensive application over a period of time which becomes possible when a task is easily within the capacity of one person.

It is easily confused with advances in (AI) big data gathering technology, capital investment or scale of operation. Division of complex process into stages may subsequently allow the development of specialised technologies for the individual stages, and this may result in specialised equipment, and hence capital investment . Similiarly, if the process is carried out with less labor and/or lower raw material costs for each unit of output, those concerned may in principle decide either the produce more . Output or the produce the same output with less input. It seems technological innovation can bring low cost benefits. In fact, new technology imposes a diseconomy on the old, eg. functions using old technology are at a cost disadvantage and must adopt or eventually disappear under free competition. So, new technology is the source of growth and adoptation in economy. The solutions to a diseconomy of scape lies in a change of scope, for example, in this case different establishments operating at different times, and perhaps with different prices. If capital investment are differentiated be improved to give longer life and better use, which in effect reduces their cost in use. For example, continuing advantages in technology allow processes to be designed in such a way that which deliver the same output with ever decreasing inputs of materials, labor or energy. Thus waste is minimised by planning and the conservation of process energy, and maintenance is reduced by change of design or the use of new materials. It may often worth spending more on equipment initially to reduce those time dependent costs. This sort of efficiency is the most obvious effect of scope rather than scale.

Deterioration and obsolescence means wear and tear are the changes which occur in artefacts as which are used , i.e. deterioration , or changes in quality or scope with time. These are not simply time effects because which depend both on the original design and on the conditions of use, such as maintenance skills and even simple care and attention. Obsolescence is difference to depreciation, it relates to the battle in the market place . The networks of markets brings products and therefore all conversion processes into competition for the same revenues. Old products will be not popular because which become harder to sell. Obsolescence, therefore depends not only on time, but also on competition, in the same time of business. It seems technological innovation can avoid obsolescence occurrence to old products to raise which competitive ability to the same markets. However, there was hardly an element in the competitive cost structures of conversion processes which was not disturbed in a way which differentiated country form country, industry from industry and firm from firm, such as (AI) big data technological innovation to any old products, which production of factor cost structures is the same basically.

8 What is the relationship between the process of (AI) big data gathering technological innovation and the production of factor?

The term "innovation" is used to describe the deliberate process by which a new product or process comes to be sold in the market. Technology innovation can be applied to conversion processes, which requires the use of energy, or their products, which have an economic energy content. It is therefore a function of all the forces which shape markets: manufacturing, processing, technology, buying, selling, information, prices costs etc. So an innovating organization may be a whole company or it may be an individual. Other forms of innovation (production of factor) relate to the sale of services within what defines as the facilitiation system. That sort of exchange is not specifically considered to be one production of factor, because it involves different adoptation processes and response times, and doesn't of itself add to the quantity of products or utilities sold.

However, invention can not be defined to one production of factor and it is to be distinguished to innovation. We can describe invention is as the process of discovering something completely new, i.e. a new fact or relationship. It is an important scientific advance. Invention enlarges the scope of man's awareness, but it doesn't necessarily have direct economic value in itself. If it is sold, it is the sale of an idea, an exchange of a little creativity for an incentive within the facilities system. It isn't marketed as a new product of a conversion process. No energy of conversion is involved. The great majority of inventions do not enter into the economic process and which do not become innovations until that happens.

If the change of scope results in a new (AI) manufacturing technological process for making a product or utility which is already being sold, this can't be differentiated from the existing product or utility in the market concerned. To be successful the new process must make it at lower unit cost than existing process. The result then is that either the price of the product fulls and processes to improve are imposed to competition or more net revenue is accumulated. So the aims of the factors of technological innovation production include: The introduction of a process for making at a lower unit cost a non-differentiated product which is sold into a commodity market, and the development and sale of a differentiated product which will draw buyers away from other markets, or draw money into the market which would not otherwise have been spent.

The nature of (AI) manufacturing technological innovation how causes factor of production. The process of technological innovation is the arrangement of materials at the elementary, say atomic or molecular level, or of components or the design of new machines, or of the relative positions of components, for example, the location of nodes in networks. There are the three levels at which the scope of the economic process may be changed. However, technological innovation can't seem without some change in the way materials ae ordered. It follows that all technological innovation flows initially from some change in a conversion process. Thus technological in the result of investment in conversion processes, where investment is defined as laying down fixed assets and so it requires a change in the use of energy consumed during conversion to make useful products. The flexible manufacturing system themselves are examples of the third level of innovation, the spatial arrangement of components and hence the link between them. Patterns of communication have changed and are continue to change as a result of new technoloby in the use of energy and the convergence of computer, data maipulation and telecommunication. Flexible manfacturing systems manufacture components in rather than having them made by supplies industries and transported to an assembly plant in batches. The new arrangements reduce both the time of reponse to market changes and all the skills of components which are needed to give flexibility of response in conventional systems , i.e. they give economy of scope.

9 How to response times in (AI) manufacturing technological innovation?

In the terminology which have developed above, the behavioral effects may be considered as adjustment of the scope of the sellers and buyers organizations as the process of acceptance of the innovation in the market proceed. Costs and risks in technological innovation, innovation requires the commitment of resources over a long period, and it is therefore subject to the same kind of risks as any investment in conversion processes. The most obvious risk is that the technological difficulties are in the initial concept, with the result that no returns will be earned and the resources sunk in the investment may have been wasted. There is a set of market-related reasons why technological success may not result in an innovation. By the time, the new process or product is ready for the market, the demand for it may have receded or may never have materialised. This may be the result of fulfiment of the potential users' needs by another technology, i.e. the innovation may be technologically obsolete before it may be because of a change of fashion or styles of living.

Two conclusions may be drawn, firstly, the product manufacturer has a good foresight and understanding is needed when undertaking projects which consume large amount of capital, or it may result in gross waste, because the future is always uncertain, however, the analysis, secondly, there is a limit to the rate of constructive innovation in an economic system, the ratio at which the system can accumulate. Hence, some product manufacturer will feel the technological innovation can be a good production of factor , such as a cost advantage is termed a competitive advantages. It is a broader term than the comparative advantages of traditional economy because of does not depend on a favorable climate or an abundance of natural resource. It is developed and maintained entirely by the skills of the people in the firms which are involved.

Technology is like on the economic process, because once knowledge about transforming inputs into outputs has been obtained, and especially after it has been implemented, it doesn't disappear. Technological innovation moves the whole process. Thus, economy of scope confer permanent advantages on those who have them. Economy of scope is to be obtained from all the elements of the economic process which change with time and these are suspectible to improvement, whether as separate elements. They involve people, and their capacity to learn and improve, and material in all their different forms.

10 Why technological innovation will be one factor of production to technological manufacture industry.

Innovation is the process by which new products' processes methods or services are created. Innovation offers added value for and users by providing better and/or cheaper functionality than previous options. Innovation combines changes in technology, business models, organization etc. The basic idea may be a new technical solutions, a new business model or a change in organization. In a competitive economy, no business can survive long term without updating its products and services or the ways in which are produced or delivered. Innovation policy must promote renewal across all business sectors and not just focus on high technological industries.

Since most innovations are complex and each subsystem has its own limitation , an important part of the innovation process is finding the right balance between conflicting demands. In most cases, there are several possible ways of providing a new function to users, or possible applications of a new technology. Which combination of features the market will prefer can't be predicted with any certainty. Whether the origin was a market opportunity on a new technological capability to one part of the production of factor to the product.

Innovation integrates knowledge from a number of different fields: technology, marketing, design, economic etc. In the production of factor view, it is hard to collect all the necessary competences in a single organization. Because technological products need to be updatd to keep competition in market. Thus, innovation has become a process of constant with suppliers and competitors, with consultants and with academic researchers. In the production of factor view, the capacity to innovate depends on how well different parts of this system are adapted to each other and how well they work together.

Today, the relationship between science and innovation is more complex and interdependent. Science-based technologies, such as microelectronics or biotechnology could not have been developed without scientific understanding, but modern science is equally dependent on advanced technology. Economists tend to prefer technology performance standards, but these risk favouring marginal improvements to existing technologies when discouraging more radical, long term solution. Also, economists tend to think of innovation as a production processes. A more production describes innovations as an experimental learning proces in which organizations and individuals build new competence. This term "research-based competence" is rather than " science-based knowledge or "scientific information".

I shall argue that economists' active process is a better way of think about the relationship between industry and academic research. Whether can the production of factor of technological innovation make use of the tools and results of research in addressing real world problem to manufacture any technological products? This main concern at the time was whether research and innovation were essentially different activities which should be supported in different ways or whether it was important to deal with both aspects together since which were interdependent. However, innovation is a process of searching, experimenting and learning. Consumers can learn about how new products, processes and services are created, how firms build competence for this and what information sources which use. So, I feel technological innovation ought be one part of production process or production of factor to some manufacturers. Such as, searching is needed for better ways of doing worth which things. Experimenting is needed because consumers can't seen in advance the best way of accomplishing a desired outcome or indeed what users really want or need. Learning is needed because actors involved in an innovation process will learn from it. The kind of learning which changes consumers' ability to solve future challenges and opportunities. However, economists often think of innovation is as a production prcocess, where knowledge transformed into a new product. We measure research and development investment, relating these to outcomes in the form of patents, new products and productivity or economic growth. Innovations are not just new technological products or processes, it also mentions organizational innovations, new distribution channels, new business models etc. In fact, it is often misleading to think about technical or organizational innovation as separate processes. Most innovations combine changes in technology, business models organization etc. in production process.

What kinds of product can belong to high technological manufacturing. For example, the world's most advanced steel plants and paper mills can never be classified as high technology because of their complementary need for high levels of investment in fixed capital, and aerospace manufacture is classified as medium technology. The standard definition of high technology measures research and development intensity not the generation or use of advanced technology as such. A far better measure is the proportion of scientists, engineers and highly qualified technicians in the labor force. For computer industry example, innovations in the field of rabotic manufacturing, nanotechnologies and human genetics research all have been enabled by low cost computational and control capabilities supplied by computers and software. Reducing the cost of software important objectives of the U.S. software industry. However, the complexity of the software industry to support the U.S. is computerized economy is increasing at an alarming rate. Software nonperformance and failure are expensive. In actuality many factors contribute to the quality issues facing the software industry. These include marketing strategies, limited liability by software vendors, and decreasing returns to testing.

At the core of these issues is the difficulty in defining and measuring software reliability, usability, efficiency, maintenability and portability. Information problems are further complicated by the fact that even with substantial testing, software developers don't truly know how their products with perform until who encounter real scenarios. The similiar industries with need have technological innovation in the productive process (production of factor), such as automotive and aerospace equipment manufacturers and related electronic communications equipment manufacturers. Quality is defined as attribute factor to different kinds of software product. Defining the attributes of software quality and determining the metrics to access the relative value of each attribute are not formalized processes. Because users place different values on each attribute depending on the product's use, it is important that quality attributes be observable to consumers. The technological innovation is one production of factor to software industry. Due to software attributes have those accurateness, interoperability, security, reliability (maturity, recoverability); usability (understandability, learnability, operability); efficiency (time behavior, resource behavior); maintainability (analyzability, changeability, stability, testability); portability (abaptability, installability, replaceability). It seems that due to software attribute have these characteristics, so it causes technological innovation is one production of factor to software industry.

Nowadays, human needs have been increasing, external factor can influence some industries cause technological innovation is one production of factor need. Together, these tends are going to reshape now human live and work, reorganize our social, economic and political institutions and redistribute power and reward in society. In the longer term, as machine learning and computer power intelligence technological innovation needs from consciousness, as machine learning and computer from consciousness, as improving health technologies allow for biological enhancements and species divergence, and as the final frontier is also needed by space travel, technological and social transformation will increasingly change what is means to be human. However, human have to better understand how our world is changing and by what forces those changes are driven . So, because human have high living quality needs, so it causes many new products have technological innovation to manufacture new product or to raise high quality need to satisfy our daily life. It will cause of factor to some products.

The (AI) manufacturing technological innovation factor can influence the economic of the pork meat production in agricultural industry. For example, the economy of the pork meat production on a farm has been carried out with the help of the method of production functions (factor- product and factor-factor). The influence of the weight of an animal on the daily growth tells us that the growth is increased with the increse of the entry weight to 19kg and with the exit weight of the fattened animal of 100 kg. So, the relationship between the daily growth and the feed costs by a feeding day shows us the tendency of than increase of a daily growth with the increase of the feed costs, e.g. with the increase of labor inputs to 2.6 hours/100 kg of the live weight and the increased profit to 29 monetary units. Labor productivity grows with the increase of the capacity usage to 87% and then it decrease.

The economy of agricultural production considerably depends on the development of cattle-breeding as a natural capacity of transforming plant products into high quality cattle products. Cattle-raising production influences the food quality, the development of food production industry, the output of high quality and healthy safe product and the development of agricultural economy. So, it seems technological innovation can be a production of factor to influence farm agricultural industry to assist farmers to apply high, e.g. agricultural technology (skills) produces high quality and tastic of farming met to satisfy consumers' diet needs.

Growth of total factor productivity (TFP) can provide society with an opportunity to increase the welfare of people. In particular, in the simplest framework, change in labor productivity factor depends on change (TFP) and capital deepening. How to change TFP? I shall suppose the technological innovation method is a factor to reduce labor cost, but it can raise labor productivity and products or goods of quality to satisfy consumers' needs in competitive market. Economists often define the knowledge economy as production and services based on knowledge-intensive activities tht contribute to an accelerated pace of technical and scientific technology, as well as rapid absolescence. Knowledge is now recognized as the driver of productivity and economic growth, leading to a new focus on the role of information, technology and learning in economic performance. In the knowledge-based economy, innovation is driven by the interaction of producers and users in the exchange of both codified and tacit knowledge: This interactive model has replaced the traditional linear model of innovation. The knowledge-intensive and high technology, economy tends to be the most dynamic in terms of output and employment growth. Changes in technology and particularly the advent of information technologies are making educated and skilled labor more valuable, and unskilled labor less. So, the technological innovation production of factor will bring skilled labor needs, more and unskilled labor needs less.

Although, it can maximize the benefits of technology for productivity, but it can raise unemployment number of non-skillful labor, because the high technological product firms will choose to dismiss the non-skillful labor and will employ skillful labor when innovation which decide to apply technological innovation method to produce whose products. For example, output and employment are expanding fastest in high technology industries, such as computers, electronic and aerospace. Also, knowledge-intensive service sectors, such as online education, communication and information(long distance call) are growing even faster, such as internet shopping technological business can be production of factor to let universities can teach students from internet, such as distance learning. Internet can be used to adventise and sell products from businessman individual website more easily. Also, mobile can use internet to do same benefits, such as laptop or desktop kinds of high technological computer products. It seems technological benefits can attract consumer individual consumption more easily. So, skillful biased technical change is a shift in the production technology that favors skilled over unskilled labor by increasing its relative productivity and therefore, its relative demand. In fact, skill-biased technical change is a shift in the production technology (factor of production that favors skilled, e.g. more relative productivity) and therefore, its relative demand.

11 How can external and internal factors affect the product and (AI) manufacturing process innovation?

In fact, the competition advantages of a company strongly depends on its possibility to benefit from innovational activities. Understanding the factors how which affect product and process innovation and their effort is necessary to be proved why innovational activities can be the one part production of factors to some new products. It has close relationship between product and business processes innovation and industry maturity and customer needs (demand) technological opportunities and investment attractiveness and company size and export orientation. These external and internal factors can influence innovational activities to some new products.

Nowadays, fast technology development, combined with the globalization and fast changes in with the globalization and fast changes in customer demand, implies that a competitive advantage of a company. So, companies will spans great effort in beating the competition innovations have a vital influence on economic development of a country. On the macro level, innovations have a vital influence on economic development that innovations are more and more present both a developed and developing countries that wish to grow developing countries that wish to grow fast and become developed. If we simply categorize companies all innovative or non-innovative. Among different innovation's categorizations is developed by researchers, the most important are: classification according to the type of innovation to degree of innovativity, innovations can be classified as incremental, semi-radical and radical innovations (Davila et al 2006), who indicates that radical innovations potentially offer huge profits and competitive advantage, but demand considerably high risk level, much company effort need and resource engagement. Otherwise, incremental innovations have more modest returns, but demand lower risk level, level of efforts and resources and are generally more successful. Finally, semi-radical innovations are somewhere between the two of them.

According to (Christensen 2003) explained to an innovations can be sustaining and disruptive. Sustaining innovations can be placed in the whole range from incremental to radical and discuptive are either semi-radical or radical. Sustaining innovations are those that improve existing products or process, disregarding the degree of improvement. Disruptive innovations create a huge growth offering a new of performances which has even it is inferior from the start comparing to existing technologies' performances a potential to become superior. Companies are advised to accept what is the best for their situation and design innovational processes, develop aptitudes, allocate resources and form partnerships in compliance to that decision.

In fact, many external and internal factors can affect companies chose product innovations, because process, innovations or their combination, e.g. factors include industry maturity, customer needs and expectations , technological opportunities, investment attractiveness, intensity of cmpetition, company size, origin of ownership and export orientation. In the industry maturity stage, as a market matures and customer needs become defined in a better way, companies transfer the focus of their competition to expenses and economy of range investing more in business processes in order to make them more effective and more efficient. Customer needs and expectations are essential for process innovations that improve process effectiveness. Orientation to customers and their satisfaction are well-known concept in the field of a total quality management.

The point of view that market demand presents the main determine the rate and activities of an invention because each rational company that tends to make profit is responsive to economic stimuli . According to Schmookler (1962) demand growth is prior to the growth in innovative activites, i.e. market requests guarantee stimuli for companies to innovate and take up new technologies. This concept is popularly called " market pull" in a sense that a market pulls innovations.

12 What is (AI) production of factor knowledge economy ?

I shall give evidences to explain why technological innovation can be one kind of production factor to some technological product manufacture industry nowadays. Nowadays, we are entering the knowledge based economy stage. Knowledge is now recognized as the driver of productivity and economic growth, leading to new focus or the role of information technology and learning in economic performance. The knowledge based economy and its relationship is as traditional economics, as reflected in " new growth theory". Because every technological product manufacturer needs workers to acquire a range of skills and to continuously adapt these skills underlines the " learning economy". The importance of knowledge and technology diffusion requires better understanding of knowledge networks and " national innovation systems".

Firstly, knowledge-based economies which are directly based on the production, distribution and use of knowledge and information. The is reflected in the trend in growth in high technology investment, high technological industries, move highly-skilled labor and associated productivity gains. Also required is tacit knowledge including the skills to use and adapt codified knowledge-based economy, innovation is driven by the interaction of producers and users in the exchange of both codified and tacit knowledge.

Employment in the knowledge-based economy is characterized by increasing demand for more highly skilled workers. The knowledge-intensive and high-technology tend to be the most dynamic in terms of output and employment growth. The science system, essentially public research laboratories and institutes of highest education, carries out key functions in the knowledge-based economy, including knowledge production, innovative technology. So, the traditional functions of producing new knowledge through basic research and educating new generations of scientists and engineers with its newer role of collaborating with industry in the transfer of knowledge and technology. For example, our societies tend to research institutes and academic increasingly have industrial partners for financial as well as innovative purposes, but most combines this with their essential role in more generic research and education.

In general, our understanding of what is happening in the knowledge-based economy is constrained by the extent and quality of the available knowledge-rated indicators. So, available knowledge-rated indicated. So, development of indicators of the knowledge-based economy must start with improvements to more traditional input indicators of research and development expenditures and research personal. Better in indicators are also needed of knowledge stocks and flows, particularly relating to the diffusion of information technologies, in both manufacturing and service sectors; social and privates rates of return to knowledge investments to the impact of innovation technology in productivity and growth.

However, knowledge is such as human being (human capital) and in innovative technology has always been central to economic development. When human is entering the 21 ST century, our output and employment are expanding tastes in high technology industries, such as computers, electronics and aerospace investment is thus being directed to high-technology products and services, particularly information and communicating technologies. Computers and related equipment are the fastest growing component of tangible investment. Equally important are more intangible investments in research and development, the training of the labor force, computer software and technical expertise. Hence, it causes employment is growing in high technology, science-based sectors ranging from computers to pharmaceuticals. Also, research and development causes manufacturing sector is losing jobs. Due to those jobs are more highly skilled and pay higher wages than those in lower technology sectors (e.g. textiles and food processing). Knowledge-based jobs in service sectors are also growing strongly. Indeed, non-production or knowledge workers those who don't engage in the output of physical products, are the employees in most demand in a wide range of activities from computer technicians, through physical therapists to marketing specialists.

Economists continue to search for the foundations of economic growth. Traditional, " production functions" focus on labor, capital , materials and energy, land; however, knowledge and technology are external influence on production. Analytical approaches are being developed. So, that knowledge can be included more directly in production functions. Investment in knowledge can raise productive capacity of the other factors of production as well as transform them into new products and processes from innovative technology.

According to the neo-classical production function, returns diminish is as more capital is added to the economy an effect which may be offset, however, by the flow of new technology. In new growth theory, knowledge can raise the returns on investment, which can contribution to the accumulation of knowledge. Technological change can also raise the relative marginal productivity of capital through education and training of the labor force, investment in research and development and the creation of new managerial structures and worth organization. In fact, incorporating knowledge into standard economic production functions is not easy task, as this factor defies some fundamental economic principles, such as that of scarcity, knowledge is intangible, but labor, capital, land, equipment etc. production of factors which can be tangible or measured. However, some kinds of knowledge can be easily reproduced and distributed at lower cost to abroad set of users, which tends to undermine private ownership. Knowledge is a much broader concept than information, which is generally the " know-what", and "know-why" components of knowledge. There are also the types of knowledge which come closet to being market commodities or economic resources to be fitted into economic production functions.

Knowledge can divide know-why and know-how both kinds of concept. Know-why means to scientific knowledge of the principles and laws of nature. This kind of knowledge underlines technological development and product and process advances in most industries. The production and reproduction of know-why is often organized in specialized organizations, such as research-laboratories and universities. Otherwise, know-how means to skills or the capability to do something. Business judging market prospects for a new product or a personnel manager selecting and training staff have to use their know-how. The same is true for the skilled worker operating complicated machine tools. Finally, knowledge-who becomes increasingly important. Know-who involves information about who knows what and who know how to do what. It involves the make if possible to get access to experts and use their knowledge efficiently. So, knowledge economy brings those conditions to our societies. One hypothesis is that globalization and international competition have led to decrease relative demand for less-skilled workers of the phenomenon; an alterative explanation is that innovative technology change has become more strongly biased in favor of skilled workers, changes in firm behavior is as the main reason for falling real wages for low-skilled workers. Thus, innovative technology and knowledge economy has close relationship to cause knowledge workers can bring high technological products of production of factor in technological product manufacture industry.

13 (AI) Production of factor internal technical skill

Secondly, it is the internal skill biased technical change influences. Skill-biased technical change is a shift in the production technology, that flavors skilled over unskilled labor by increasing its relative productivity and , therefore, its relative demand of innovative technology of production factor. The direction of technical changes i.e. whether new capital complements skilled or unskilled labor may be determined by innovators' economic incentives shaped by relative prices, the size of the market and institutions.

Economic theory views the production technology as a function describing that a collection of factor inputs can be transformed into output, and it defines technical change as a shift in the production of function. In fact, given who observed movements of the production function only concentrates on , such as land supply, labor numbers, equipment supply, capital demand factors. Therefore,To make sense of these recent developments, the concept of factor biased technical change can be another production of factor to influence the new technical products quantities change. For example, the timing of the rise in the skill premium has changed the rapid diffusion of information and communication technologies in the workplace environment in any high technological industry generally nowadays. For example, expenditures in information processing equipment and software, is as a share of U.S. private non-residential fixed investment, rose from 6% in 1960 year to 40% in 2000 year. At the heart of those dynamic change.

This is an improvement in the quality and productivity of all those equipment products, relying heavily on semiconductors like computers, software and switching equipment underlying much of communication technology. In the early adoption phase of a new technology, that those who adapt more quickly can reap some benefits. As time goes by, there will be enough makers learning how to work with the new technology to offset the wage differential. Note the difference with the hypothesis set, where the effect of capital deepening on the skill premium is permanent. Also, information technologies production of factor can reduce costs of data storage, communication, monitoring and supervision activities within the firm which causes a shift towards a new organizational design. In particular, the layers in the hierarchical structure can be reduced, so that the organization of the firm becomes "flatter". So, workers no longer perform routinized, responsible for a wide range of tasks within teams. Therefore, adaptable workers verses at multi-tasking activities benefits is a factor of production to reduce internal cost of any firms.

Due to technological innovation causes the layers in the hierarchical structure can be reduced, so that the organization of the firm becomes "flatter". How technological innovation can influence internal skill biased technical change to orgnizational structure. Development behavioral means it is through managment theory. So, high technological skillful organization will choose to apply theory x more than theory y because this technological innovation will reduce some unskillful staffs and give more effort and duties to those skillful staffs to use high technological skill to do whose jobs daily and who will feel lazy and unhappy to do extra more technological jobs. Theory x assumptions are the average human being dislike of work and work avoid if who can, most people must be controlled, directed or threatened with punishment to adequate effort to action organization objective; otherwise, theory y assumptions are people like to use physical and mental effort to work as natural as play and rest, human being dislike work, a source of satisfaction, threat of punishment are not being effort. Hence, technological innovation can cause organizations to change whose structure and skill staffs need to do more jobs. It causes employer need to give extristic and intrinsic motivations to satisfy whose skillful staffs needs to raise efficiency, e.g. giving more tangible reward, as salary, benefit, security, promotion, good contract of condition of work service, comfortable workplace environment as well as using one ability to achieve who feel apprecation, positive being treating of psychological satisfactory needs.

In technological innovation of organization structure, the management committee needs to concern whose skillful technological labor individual psychological needs. Because technological innovation is one important production of factor and it has close relationship between motivation and staff individual efficiency and productivity. As Maslow's hierarchy of needs indicates people (staffs) mean having satisfied to achieve motivation behavior, the lowest love is basic physiological, the need for food, as salary, safe working condition, then is job security, benefit. Next is friendship at work group, after is promotion, payment increasing, high status of job title. Finally is achievement in work advancement opportunitie creative task in related aspect at work motivation. Hence, after the traditional non-technological innoviation of organization changed the technological innovation of organizational structure, management needs to concern that motivation is needed to develop of behavioral through contributed to management theory. Every organiztion manageer needs to know what its team staffs whose indvidual needs, it includes extrinsic needs, e.g. salary, promotion, security as well as intrinsic needs, e.g. achievement, appreciaton. If the employees feel extrinsic needs are more than intrinsic needs, the managers can consider what extrinsic needs, the managers can consider what extrinsic needs of whose employee individual need. If the employee feels intrinsic needs are more than extrinsic needs, the manage can consider what intrinsic needs the employee individual actual need in order to motivate the skillful worker to work efficiently and raising productivity.

After changing the technological innovation of organizational structure, the management needs to concern how to plan to raise its productivity from its production of factor of technological innovation. Planning is looking ahead, control is looking back, every organization must need strategic plan, operative plan and tastic plan for every department to give aim for its mission objectives. Then it needs to achieve its any short term plans or long term plans efficiently, e.g. how to achieve to produce and to sell 5,000 computers sale objective or how to increase to achieve 20% profit or productivity objective from 10% within one year. So, after the technological innovation production of factor influences the organization needs to find reasons what how to influence it can not achieve these new objectives within one year. Then, it needs to find reasons and revises to solve challenges to control it can achieve it's planning objectives. For example, SWOT method indicates what its internal strengths and weaknesses, external threats and opportunities are. To aim achieve its planning strategic plan every year. Before the organization is not technological innovation, it can't have control is looking ahead, due to planning is looking back because organization can;t know what it's mission and objectives can't achieve to revise if it has no any strategic plan, operational plan and tactical plan for top, middle and low level to let different department managers to know what it's mission and objectives are planned to achieve before the organization has not changed the technological innovation of organizational structure in the year. Besides, after the technological innovation changed the organizational structure. The management needs to concern how to implement it's strategies effectively. The technological innovation of organization needs to change its old long term strategic plan to be new long term strategic plan in the top level, e.g. one year what is its new mission for its technologcial innovation, e.g. Apple brand of computer company needs to innovate its old style computer design to know how to adapt the young client group needs (demand) in this competitive computer technological product industry.

Finally, after innovative organizational structure, mangement needs to concern how to raise skillful labor individual productivity and efficiency, due to who need to increase more effort to do their jobs after technological innovation. I shall indicate on job training method. The advantages on limitations of different approaches to on the job training include the company needs to spend extra time and resources to train staffs or workers to work, when who are on the regular work time. Hence, it will lose staffs to do regular job duties, due who needs to learn how to do their job. So the employer needs to pay higher salary to every job trainer for long term if it needs to train many skillful labor after technological innovation. It can't ensure whether the training employees can work efficiently and know who are not the right staffs to get training. Hence, it will employ the staffs who are not right staffs to accept job training riskly if the mangement have not evaluate who have effort to be train to raise whose productivity and testing personal effort of evaluation is more important to the job trainers.

14 What are the (AI) technical change as exogenous or endogenous production of factor?

Finally, I shall indicate what the change is as exogenous or endogenous factor in the (AI) production function model to cause innovative technology to produce new technological product in manufacture industry. Although, economic theory firstly treated technology change is as a residual, the unexplained part remaining after the contribution of an increased quantity and quality of capital, labor and natural resources in output growth have been accounted for. However, the theory of economic growth reconsidered recently the nature of technological change and the concept of knowledge. Therefore, the new growth economic theory includes research and development is as a factor of influence in the macroeconomic models.

The endogenous or exogenous nature of technological change refers to its source: endogenous is internal to the national economy, being created by domestic private or public enterprise, when exogenous change is external originating from foreign sources. So, it seems research and development workforce is as new factor in the production function model. Although, technological progress, managerial improvements and innovation in general are nowadays largely regarded as key contributors to economic growth. Schumpeter (1939) defines technical progress in terms of production function, which describes the way the production output varies according to the quantity and quality of the input factors. So, the technological change represents the factor that shifts the production function.

From the theoretical viewpoint, it has difficult to separate knowledge from the other factors of the production function. The total labor factor productivity is usually estimated by output the capital and labor factors, weighted by their specific shares. Under perfect competition, the price of the production factors is equal to their marginal productivity, hence, their shares in outputs are equal to their exponents from the production function.

Otherwise, from the empirical point of view, there are difficulties of measurement, especially in the case of value added and research-development variables. So, from all available data on research and development input and outputs, research and development expenditures are most frequently used, along with the number of patents, the technological balance of payments, machinery and tools inputs etc. costs to measure of input in innovation.

Furthermore, the exponents of the new growth theory indicates modeled knowledge is as an output quality of the research and development sector and proved that contrary to the neoclassical conclusions of the diminishing-returns technology, the introduction of the human capital changes the production function into one with increasing returns. Thus, it seems total research and development expenditures are used in this model as a measure of total investments (material and intangible) in the research and development sector. However, in many studies, the research and development stock is calculated as the accumulated value of research and development expenditure after depreciation, a procedure which implies the assumption that all of the research and development expenditure certainly and that it's stock depreciates with a certain fixed rate. Since, long time-series data on R & D are rarely available, other studies assume that the growth rate of R & D expenditure to R & D stock is stable. Hence in innovation technological industry, the labor production factor can be divided into two components total employees population outside the research development sector and the number of employees in research and development. The same types of division was applied to the capital production factor.

Reference

Christensen, C.M. (2003) " the innovator's dilema", Harpercollins, New York.

Davila, T., Epstein, M. J., Shelton.R. (2006) " Making innovation work: How to manage it, measure it and profit from it". Warton school publishing, New Jersey.

Schmookler, J., (1962) " Economic sources of incentive activity, " the journal of economic history. vol. 22
, no. 1 (Mar. 1962), 1-20.

Schumpeter, J., A. (1939), business cycles: A Theoretical Historical And Statistical Analysis Of Capitalist Processes, New York: Macmillan.

Reference

Future of jobs survey, World Economic Forum.
Hauser, J. Tellis, G. J; Griffin, A. 2006. Research On Innovation: A Review And Agenda For Marketing Science. 25(6): 687-717.

J.P. Holdren & P.R. Enrlich, " Human population and the global environment", American Scientist, vol. 62 (1974), pp.282-92.
Joel E. Cohen, How many people can the earth support? (New York: Norton, 1995), pp. 212-36, 261-62.
Mohr, G. J. Griffin, A. 2010. Research On Innovation : A Review And Agenda For Marketing Science. 25 (6): 687-717.
Names of drivers have abbreviated to ensure legibility. Future of jobs survey, World Economic Forum.
" Presence to prosperity", PWC Growth Markets Centre Report: http://www.pwc.com/gx/en/growth-markets-centre/presence-to-profitability.jhtml

9 798888 091240